POST STRUCTURAL- ISM AND THE NEW TESTAMENT

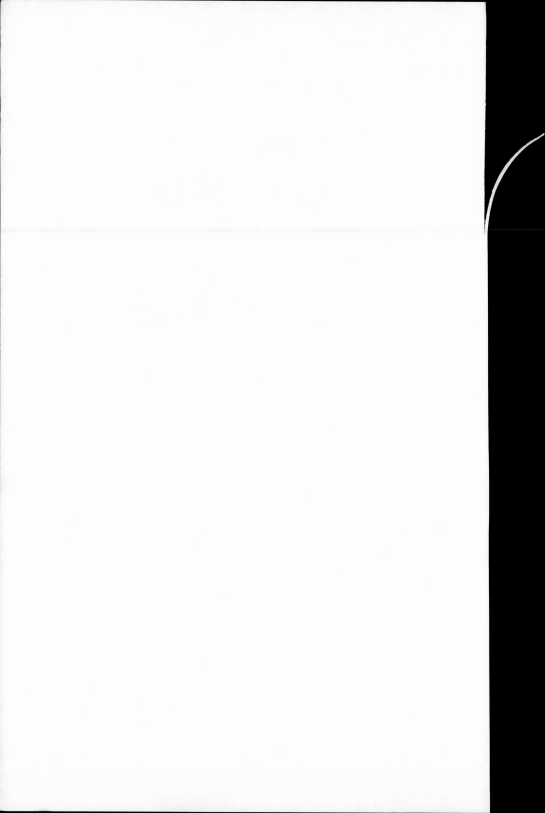

POST STRUCTURAL- ISM AND THE NEW TESTAMENT

Derrida

and

Foucault

at the

Foot of

the Cross

STEPHEN D. MOORE

FORTRESS PRESS
Minneapolis

In memory of my father
and in celebration of my daughter

POSTSTRUCTURALISM AND THE NEW TESTAMENT
Derrida and Foucault at the Foot of the Cross

Portions of chapter 2 are based in part on the author's article "Are There Impurities in the Living Water That the Johanine Jesus Dispenses?" in *Biblical Interpretation* 1:2 (1993). Used by permission of E. J. Brill. Portions of chapter 3 are based in part on the author's article " 'Mirror, Mirror, . . .' " in *Semeia* 62 (1993). Used by permission of Scholars Press. Portions of chapter 5 are based in part on the author's previous publication, "God's Own (Pri)son," in Francis Watson, ed. *The Open Text* (London: SCM Press, LTD, 1993). Used by permission.

Scripture quotations in English, except where noted, are from the New Revised Standard Version of the Bible, copyright © 1989 by the Division of Christian Education of the National Council of Churches of Christ in the USA and are used by permission. Greek quotations from the New Testament follow the Nestle-Aland twenty-sixth revised edition, copyright © 1983 by the United Bible Societies.

Cover design: Ann Elliot Artz Hadland
Cover image: *Black Glass Still Life with Fish, Pear and Skeleton* by Steve Hawley, copyright © 1990.

Library of Congress Cataloging-in-Publication Data

Moore, Stephen D., 1954–
    Poststructuralism and the New Testament : Derrida and Foucault at
the foot of the Cross / Stephen D. Moore.
        p.   cm.
    Includes bibliographical references.
    ISBN 0-8006-2599-4 (alk. paper) :
    1. Bible. N.T.—Criticism, interpretation, etc. 2. Derrida,
Jacques—Influence. 3. Foucault, Michel—Influence.
    4. Deconstruction. I. Title.
BS2377.6.M66   1994
225.6—dc20   94-2954
                                                                   CIP

Manufactured in the U.S.A.   AF 1-2599

98   97   96   95   94   1   2   3   4   5   6   7   8   9   10

CONTENTS

ACKNOWLEDGMENTS

My baby daughter, Olivia, tried hard to prevent this book from being published. Eventually she relented and taught me how to write while baby-sitting. My wife, Jane Hurwitz, helped even more by frequently enabling me to write while not baby-sitting. Along the way, I test-read two chapters of the book to the Duke Divinity School community; my special thanks to Dale Martin and Steve Long who made it possible, and to Regina Schwartz and Elizabeth Clark who helped make it so pleasurable. Nearer home, my campus support group, Theorists Anonymous, lent a sympathetic ear to another chapter and offered therapeutic advice; my thanks to Drs. Berger and Veeser in particular. Others, too, at various times and in various ways, supplied vital encouragement, or insightful suggestions that I gratefully incorporated, or would have had I had the energy, notably Janice Capel Anderson, Cheryl Exum, D. Moody Smith, Sandra Schneiders, and Francis Watson. Most of all, I wish to thank Marshall Johnson of Fortress Press, who commissioned this book and supported it from its first stumbling steps to its final shambling strides.

INTRODUCTION:
A (PERSONAL) HISTORY
OF POSTSTRUCTURALISM

*"Would you describe your work as structuralist?" I ventured nervously.
"Post-structuralist, I should hope," she answered testily. That was my
very first encounter with the word. It was in December of 1982, ten
years ago this month.*

What better way to get a handle on poststructuralism than to
ask a leading poststructuralist how it all began? An interviewer once
put the question to Michel Foucault. "What is the origin of what we
loosely call Post-Structuralism?" he inquired, poised, presumably, for
an exhaustive account. "Indeed, why not this term?" replied Foucault.[1]

*Shyly, I asked her to recommend a good entrée to poststructuralism.
Sagely, she suggested* Of Grammatology *by somebody named Jacques
Derrida.*

Foucault's phlegmatic retort was an expression of Foucauldian
theory, which is outlined in chapter 4. Suffice it for now to note that
Foucault's point was that it is the term *poststructuralism* itself (shorthand for the sprawling discourse on poststructuralism) that brings the
phenomenon poststructuralism into view, complete with birth certif-
icate, passport, and curriculum vitae. Once we have hooked this term
around our ears, balanced it on our nose, we begin to see poststructuralism in all the appropriate places—in critiques or extensions of

1. Michel Foucault, "How Much Does It Cost for Reason to Tell the
Truth?" in *Foucault Live (Interviews, 1966–84)*, ed. Sylvère Lotringer, trans.
John Johnston (New York: Semiotext[e], 1989), 233.

structuralism, for example. Notable among such critiques or revisions were those undertaken in France in the late 1960s by Jacques Derrida, Roland Barthes, Julia Kristeva, and others.[2] At the time, however, there was no French term in use corresponding to the English term *poststructuralism*, nor did the English term exist at that early date. The term was coined some time later in the United States—when, where, or by whom nobody seems to know, except that by the late 1970s it was being passed from hand to hand in French and English departments across the country. Thus, the term was quite "unknown in France until its 'return' from the United States," as Derrida would later put it.[3]

I had hurt myself on structuralism the previous semester, carelessly delving into books with such enticing titles as The New Testament and Structuralism, *only to be beaten back by a wild flurry of neologisms and an impenetrable phalanx of semiotic squares.*

Poststructuralism can justly be said to have been implicit in structuralism from the latter's inception. More than anything else, French structuralism was an attempt to extend the methodological principles of Ferdinand de Saussure, the "father" of modern linguistics, to a broad range of academic disciplines— anthropology, literary studies, psychology, history, cultural studies, and political science, to name but a few.[4] As we shall see in chapter 1, however, Saussure's structural linguistics, pressed to their logical conclusion, quickly became something that Saussure himself could not have foreseen: a general philosophy of language with disturbing ramifications for philosophy in general, not to mention theology, as well as literary criticism and numerous other fields, biblical studies included.

Today the term *poststructuralism* conjures up a litany of names—preeminently the unholy trinity of Derrida, Foucault, and Jacques Lacan, with Barthes, Kristeva, and other assorted eminences

2. See, e.g., Jacques Derrida, "Structure, Sign, and Play in the Discourse of the Human Sciences," in *Writing and Difference*, trans. Alan Bass (Chicago: University of Chicago Press, 1978), 278–93; Roland Barthes, *S/Z*, trans. Richard Miller (New York: Hill and Wang, 1974); and Julia Kristeva, *Séméiotiké: Recherches pour une sémanalyse* (Paris: Seuil, 1969).

3. Jacques Derrida, "Letter to a Japanese Friend," in *Derrida and Différance*, ed. David Wood and Robert Bernasconi (Evanston, Ill.: Northwestern University Press, 1988), 3.

4. See Glossary. For a more detailed account, see Daniel Patte, *Structural Exegesis for New Testament Critics* (Minneapolis: Fortress Press, 1990).

trailing close behind. More precisely, the term summons up a host of diverse and distinctive projects:

▶ Derrida's philosophical project, best known as *deconstruction* (which will be the topic of chapter 1)

▶ deconstructive literary criticism, essentially an American product, inspired by Derrida's readings of literary and philosophical texts, but also by those of Paul de Man, who was principal of the school of deconstruction that flourished at Yale in the 1970s and early 1980s[5]

▶ certain of Barthes's writings, especially his later ones, which exuberantly blur the boundaries between criticism and literature[6]

▶ Lacan's "return to Freud," specifically, Freud's unsettling early vision of the human subject as irremediably split or disunified (which I discuss in chapter 3)

▶ Kristeva's seminal work on intertextuality[7]

▶ Foucault's work on power (which I discuss in chapter 4 and harness in chapter 5)

and so on.

As this shortlist suggests, *poststructuralism* is a more expansive umbrella term than *deconstruction*; the latter term is normally reserved for the work of Derrida, de Man, and those who draw on them, whereas all the items on my list would generally be termed poststructuralist. Finally, the fact that Lacan, Foucault, and Barthes were deemed arch-structuralists in the 1960s (in Lacan's case, on the basis of the very same work that would later be dubbed poststructuralist) underscores yet again the symbiotic relationship between structuralism and poststructuralism—an inevitable symbiosis, given the incestuousness of Parisian intellectual life in the 1960s (Derrida was a disaffected student of Foucault, Kristeva an admiring student of Barthes, all four attendees at Lacan's famous seminar, and so on).

5. See Glossary for a more detailed encapsulation of deconstruction, and Further Reading for a selected bibliography.

6. See, e.g., Roland Barthes, *The Pleasure of the Text*, trans. Richard Miller (New York: Hill and Wang, 1975); *Roland Barthes by Roland Barthes*, trans. Richard Howard (New York: Hill and Wang, 1977); *A Lover's Discourse: Fragments*, trans. Richard Howard (New York: Hill and Wang, 1978); and *Camera Lucida: Reflections on Photography*, trans. Richard Howard (New York: Hill and Wang, 1981). Barthes's *S/Z* is often said to have ushered in this period of his work.

7. See Glossary and Further Reading.

The next day I tracked down Of Grammatology *in the library. Accustomed as I was then to seeking a Word from the Lord, I opened it at random and began to read*:

> It is because arche-writing, movement of differance, irreducible arche-synthesis, opening in one and the same possibility, temporalization as well as relationship with the other and language, cannot, as the condition of all linguistic systems, form a part of the linguistic system itself and be situated as an object in its field. (Which does not mean it has a real field elsewhere, another assignable site.)[8]

I replaced the book with a shudder and a sigh. As I did so, my eyes locked on another book with the intriguing title, Reader-Response Criticism. *Thus it was that I wrote my dissertation on the role of the reader in Luke-Acts.*

If all the extant introductions to particular poststructuralists, or to poststructuralism in general, were laid end to end, they would encircle Paris several times. Since the secondary lit(t)erature is already excessive, therefore (despite endless recycling), my own little book need not pretend to be comprehensive.[9] I propose to limit myself largely to Derrida and Foucault, with an occasional glance at Lacan.

8. Jacques Derrida, *Of Grammatology*, trans. Gayatri Chakravorty Spivak (Baltimore: Johns Hopkins University Press, 1976), 60, his emphasis.

9. Much more comprehensive are Richard Harland, *Superstructuralism: The Philosophy of Structuralism and Post-Structuralism* (New York: Methuen, 1987); Peter Dews, *Logics of Disintegration: Poststructuralist Thought and the Claims of Critical Theory* (London: Verso, 1987); and Art Berman, *From the New Criticism to Deconstruction: The Reception of Structuralism and Post-Structuralism* (Urbana and Chicago: University of Illinois Press, 1988). More accessible than these are John Sturrock, ed., *Structuralism and Since: From Lévi-Strauss to Derrida* (New York: Oxford University Press, 1979), and Madan Sarup, *An Introductory Guide to Post-Structuralism and Postmodernism* (Athens: University of Georgia Press, 1989). More advanced, but suggestive for biblical exegesis, are Derek Attridge, Geoff Bennington, and Robert Young, eds., *Post-Structuralism and the Question of History* (New York: Cambridge University Press, 1987), and Richard Machin and Christopher Norris, eds., *Post-Structuralist Readings of English Poetry* (New York: Cambridge University Press, 1987). Still more suggestive, perhaps, are Gary A. Phillips, ed., *Poststructural Criticism and the Bible: Text/History/Discourse* (*Semeia* 51; Atlanta: Scholars Press, 1990); David Jobling and Stephen D. Moore, eds., *Poststructuralism as Exegesis* (*Semeia* 54; Atlanta: Scholars Press, 1991); and Stephen D. Moore, *Mark and Luke in Poststructuralist Perspectives: Jesus Begins to Write* (New Haven, Conn.: Yale University Press, 1992).

Why Derrida and Foucault? For two related reasons. First, because these two thinkers have been more widely taught, read, read about, written upon—or written off—than any of their French poststructuralist peers (Barthes and Lacan included, although their impact too on Anglo-American academe has been considerable). Second, because I am impatient to see the new literary criticism of the New Testament finally come to terms with secular literary criticism as it really is, and has been for nearly two decades—which to say, far more often informed by Derridean or Foucauldian poststructuralism than by structuralist narratology or reader-response theory. (The architects of the new literary criticism of the Gospels have drawn their blueprints mainly from the latter two areas.)[10] Derrida's early writings had a remarkable impact on American literary studies in the 1970s and early 1980s (I discuss this in chapter 1), while Foucault's later writings, culminating in his multivolume *History of Sexuality*, have had a comparable impact on the discipline since the early 1980s, fueling such important innovations as the New Historicism and the still-nascent field of gender studies.[11]

Reader-response criticism proved to be a slippery slope that eventually plunged me into poststructuralism.[12] *Today I cannot read a reader-oriented reading of a Gospel without feeling that it is an inadvertent caricature of redaction criticism. Many of the standard moves of redaction criticism are retained in reader-response criticism, but are*

10. I am referring to such critics as Alan Culpepper, Jack Dean Kingsbury, David Rhoads, Robert Tannehill, and Robert Fowler.
11. On New Historicism, see Further Reading. On gender studies, a field that encompasses the study of gender construction, masculine and feminine, as well as gay and lesbian studies, see Elaine Showalter, ed., *Speaking of Gender* (New York: Routledge, 1989); Eve Kosofsky Sedgwick, "Gender Criticism," in *Redrawing the Boundaries: The Transformation of English and American Literary Studies,* ed. Stephen Greenblatt and Giles Gunn (New York: Modern Language Association, 1992), 271–302; and Naomi A. Schor, "Feminist and Gender Studies," in *Introduction to Scholarship in Modern Languages and Literatures,* ed. Joseph Gibaldi (2d ed.; New York: Modern Language Association, 1992), 262–87. For Foucault's influence on New Historicism, see Judith Newton, "Historicisms New and Old: 'Charles Dickens' Meets Marxism, Feminism, and West Coast Foucault," *Feminist Studies* 16 (1990): 449–70; and for his influence on gender studies, see Sedgwick, "Gender Criticism," 278–94; and Schor, "Feminist and Gender Studies," 277–79.
12. See Glossary for a definition of reader-response criticism.

accentuated to the point of parody. To this extent, the redaction critic is a reader-response critic who has yet to come out of the closet. For the redaction critic has always been faced with the challenge of enacting a hypothetical role of reading, of becoming the ideal reader or hearer of a Gospel, of becoming attuned to the subtleties of the evangelist's intentions. This implicit agenda becomes fully explicit in reader-response criticism. The reader-response critic spins out a full-fledged story of reading, one whose hero/ine is the implied reader, and whose plot is made up of this reader's successive attempts to negotiate the gaps, ambiguities, and enigmas of the Gospel text.[13]

In consequence, I quickly found that the reader-oriented reading, far from being an enterprise qualitatively different from the narrative it is commenting on, tended to be disconcertingly similar to it. For the implied reader is, in the final analysis, a fictional character in a fictional narrative, a story of reading that is hopelessly tangled up in the Gospel narrative it is supposed to be disentangling. As such, reader-response criticism enacts and reenacts the collapse of critical "metalanguage"[14]*—the pretensions of one form of language (criticism) to pronounce on another form of language (literature) from a position safely outside or above it. But just as redaction criticism opens out onto reader-response criticism, what was implicit in the former becoming explicit in the latter, so too does reader-response criticism open out onto poststructuralism, since the impossibility of metalanguage is a recurrent poststructuralist theme. In part, poststructuralism*

> *is a critique of the view that one could get outside and above a domain one was describing. The term poststructuralism would thus most accurately be used to designate the claim that structuralist [and other sorts of] analyses are caught up in the processes and mechanisms they are analyzing.*
>
> *The most familiar example of this, of course, is the way in which any analysis of, say, the political forces in a society cannot*

13. Jonathan Culler first impelled me to think this through; see *On Deconstruction: Theory and Criticism after Structuralism* (Ithaca, N.Y.: Cornell University Press, 1982), 64–83.

14. "[T]his word designates a language which speaks of another language. If, for instance, I am writing a grammar of the French language, I produce a metalanguage, since I am speaking a language (to wit, my grammar) about a language which is French" (Roland Barthes, "The Structural Analysis of Narrative: Apropos of Acts 10–11," in *The Semiotic Challenge*, trans. Richard Howard [New York: Hill and Wang, 1988], 237).

situate itself outside of the realm of political forces; it is necessarily caught up in the processes, affected by the forces it is describing, and itself involves a political move or stance. Thus, one way to study the political forces at work would be to analyze the analyst's own stance and investigate how his or her analytical discourse is worked by the forces it is analyzing. This is the poststructuralist move.[15]

In order to avoid madness and complete my dissertation, I was obliged to herd all such considerations into an Appendix. Later they escaped to become a book.

In my chapters on deconstruction in the present book, I am out to deflect two charges that have often been hurled against it. The first is that deconstruction is utterly inimical to theological concerns. I attempt to elucidate Derrida's philosophical project in chapter 1 (the most demanding chapter in the book), and to show in the process that he has always been in a muted dialogue with theology—specifically, with that marginalized strand of it known as negative theology.

The second charge is that deconstruction is apolitical—unable or unwilling to engage with such issues as social inequality (issues of gender, race, class, and so forth). The simple answer to this charge is that deconstruction is as political as one wants it to be (I discuss this further in chapter 1). These days I find I am learning more from feminist critics of the Bible than from any other group of biblical scholars; in consequence, chapter 2 finds me struggling to bring deconstruction and feminism into dialogue around a certain well in Samaria, where Jesus and a woman are already in conversation.

Reader-response criticism plunged me into poststructuralism in other ways as well. To perform a reader-oriented reading of a Gospel is to split, ameobalike, into (at least) two persons or personae. Your own jaded responses to this overread text must be systematically repressed in order to allow the reader-in-the-text to emerge, a hypothetical reader, who, unlike you, is encountering the text for the first time and is capable of being shocked and surprised by its unexpected twists and turns, a reader whose responses are "exemplary," unlike your own, wholly obedient to the law of the text—in short, a reader who is an extension of you, but by no means identical with you. Here too the reader-response critic is waltzing with poststructuralism without knowing it.

15. Jonathan Culler, "Poststructuralist Criticism," *Style* 21 (1987): 173.

For poststructuralism, like structuralism, entails a stringent critique of the humanist concept of a unified self, as I explain in chapter 3.

Chapter 3 further extends deconstruction's encounter with biblical criticism. In particular I attempt to examine deconstruction's odd affinity with the "old" literary criticism of the Gospels (epitomized by source criticism), and its lack of affinity with the new (epitomized by narrative criticism).

Chapter 4 switches from deconstruction to Foucault. Having introduced Foucault in chapter 4, I take my lead from him in chapter 5 in order to defamiliarize an overly familiar—and oddly violent—symbol of the Christian faith, namely the cross, which casts its shadow over so much of the New Testament, the letters of Paul in particular.

As far as I am concerned personally, my reading of John and his interpreters, on the one hand, and Paul and his interpreters, on the other, are the make-or-break chapters of this book. Temperamentally, each of these readings gives expression to a hermeneutics of suspicion, if not a hermeneutics of paranoia. Methodologically, however, they have little in common. The first is a close reading of some portions of a New Testament text, the second is not; rather it is an attempt to expose the ideology of a certain brand of Christian soteriology, and it ranges all the way from the Gospels and Paul to medieval and modern theology. The methodological disparity between the two readings reflects some of the differences between Derrida and Foucault. Derrida seldom writes anything that is not a close reading of some other writing. He writes best curled up in someone else's text; hence his interest for literary critics, and for us, even though his parent field is philosophy. Foucault, too, can be classed as a philosopher, although most of his books look like histories (he himself implied more than once that they are actually parodies of standard historiography).[16] He tends to work with texts in the manner of a historian; he rarely engages in a sustained reading of a single text, preferring to roam over a wide range of sources.

The upshot of what I am saying is that no single method of reading is espoused in this book, nor can it be. Derrida and Foucault

16. See, e.g., Michel Foucault, "The History of Sexuality," in *Power/Knowledge: Selected Interviews and Other Writings 1972–1977*, ed. Colin Gordon, trans. Colin Gordon et al. (New York: Pantheon Books, 1980), 193, and "The Discourse of History," in *Foucault Live*, 20.

each employ very different strategies of reading, and other leading poststructuralists (Barthes, Lacan, de Man, et al.) have their own distinctive tactics in addition. A further complication arises from the fact that deconstruction is congenitally suspicious of the concept of method itself. The implicit narrative of deconstruction, particularly in its American manifestations, concerns a contest between criticism and literature. According to the standard story line, literature *is* that which perenially resists the colonizing ambitions of method, as we shall see in chapter 2. (Rumors of literature's death at the hands of deconstruction are therefore greatly exaggerated.)

All of this presents unusual, not to say impossible, problems for the writer of a methodological guide. To counterbalance these debilitating complications, I pampered and fed my two exegetical examples until they became a strapping pair of nonidentical twins eager to carry the burden of this book on their shoulders—that of showing that poststructuralism is worth pursuing even if at first difficult to grasp. For even as it slips away shyly, quietly shutting the door behind it, it opens up promising new perspectives on old New Testament texts and themes.

Later I discovered that the stylistic sadist who had whipped me with "It is because arche-writing, movement of differance, irreducible arche-synthesis," and so on, could also write astonishingly visceral prose. How about this for a mouthful, for example:

> *The membranous partition that is called the soft palate, fixed by its upper edge to the limit of the vault, freely floats, at its lower edge, over the base of the tongue. Its two lateral edges (it has four sides) are called "pillars." In the middle of the floating edge, at the entrance to the throat, hangs the fleshy appendix of the uvula, like a small grape.* The text is spit out. *It is like a discourse whose unities are molded in the manner of an excrement, a secretion. . . . [S]aliva is the element that . . . glues the unities to one another.*[17]

Derrida's anatomically correct prose impels me to imagine an Anatomy of the Fourth Gospel *that would read—and bleed—like* Gray's Anatomy, *a fittingly fleshly receptacle for critical reflection on the Gospel of the incarnate God. This too is "poststructuralism."*

---

17. Jacques Derrida, *Glas*, trans. John P. Leavey, Jr., and Richard Rand (Lincoln: University of Nebraska Press, 1986), 142b, emphasis added.

PART ONE
DERRIDA

1
DECONSTRUCTION, THEOLOGY, AND THE *DIFFÉRANCE* BETWEEN THEM

> [Deconstruction] has been called, precipitately, a type of negative theology (this was neither true nor false . . .).
>
> —*Jacques Derrida*[1]

CRUCIAL TO Derrida's philosophical project is a strategic recasting of the structural linguistics of Ferdinand de Saussure. To put it another way, Saussure's *Cours de linguistique générale*, suitably boosted, is an indispensable part of the Derridean can(n)on.[2] Indeed, as I have already hinted, Saussure's general significance for French structuralism and poststructuralism alike can hardly be overstated.[3] A

---

1. Derrida, "Letter to a Japanese Friend," 3.
2. Ferdinand de Saussure, *Cours de linguistique générale*, ed. Charles Balley and Albert Sechehaye, in collaboration with Albert Riedlinger (5th ed.; Paris: Editions Payot, 1955); trans. Roy Harris as *Course in General Linguistics* (La Salle, Ill.: Open Court, 1986).
3. Roland Barthes, for example, recalling the beginning of his structuralist "adventure" in the 1950s, declares: "It was then that I first read Saussure; and having read Saussure, I was dazzled by this hope: to give my denunciation of the self-proclaimed petit-bourgeois myths the means of developing scientifically" ("Introduction: The Semiological Adventure," in *The Semiotic Challenge*, 5). Saussure was no less a luminous discovery for other structuralists and poststructuralists also, notably Claude Lévi-Strauss and Jacques Lacan.

crash course in the *Cours* is therefore in order. The collision will carry us into Derrida, and beyond that into negative theology.

A CRASH *COURS* IN SAUSSURE

"For some people," complains Saussure, "a language, reduced to its essentials, is a nomenclature: a list of terms corresponding to a list of things."[4] "This conception is open to a number of objections," however, not least being the fact that "it leads one to assume that the link between a name and a thing is something quite unproblematic, which is far from being the case."[5] "A linguistic sign is not a link between a thing and a name," insists Saussure, "but between a concept and a sound pattern" (a sound as processed by a hearer).[6] With a flourish, he declares that he will replace the terms *sound pattern* and *concept* with *signifier* and *signified*, respectively, and retain the term *sign* to designate the two combined.[7] The signifier, then, would be the material (acoustic) component of the sign as it registers in the mind of the hearer (the sound *tree*, for example), while the signified would be the sign's conceptual component (the concept *tree*). However, given that Saussure's sound pattern-become-signifier is already a quasi-conceptual quantity—sound as processed in the mind of the hearer as opposed to unprocessed sound waves (those produced by the proverbial tree that falls unheard by any human ear)—we may well ask what the real difference is between a sound pattern and a concept, between a signifier and a signified. As we shall soon see, to begin to ask such questions is to set foot on the forest path that leads to the precipice of poststructuralism.

Note, incidentally, that Saussure's account of the linguistic sign brackets the "thing" or referent altogether (in this case, a large perennial plant commonly exceeding ten feet in height), not because he doubts its existence—to do so would be to risk a concussion—but

---

4. Saussure, *Course in General Linguistics*, 65. The "Saussure" who speaks here is actually a critical construct. Saussure died in 1913 without leaving a detailed written account of his theories. The *Cours de linguistique générale*, first published in 1916, was put together largely from lecture notes taken by Saussure's pupils at the University of Geneva.

5. Ibid., 65–66.

6. Ibid., 66.

7. Ibid., 67.

because it is not part of the internal structure of language. "The linguist must take the study of linguistic structure as his primary concern," asserts Saussure.[8]

The structure of language, for Saussure, is also the structure of thought. Apart from language, thought is chaotic: "In itself, thought is like a swirling cloud, where no shape is intrinsically determinate. No ideas are established in advance, and nothing is distinct, before the introduction of linguistic structure."[9] (The comparison with Genesis is irresistible: "In the beginning . . . the earth was a formless void. . . . Then God said . . . and there was. . . .") Structured thought cannot exist before language; in consequence, language cannot be regarded as a mere instrument, something one uses to "express one's thoughts." Thought and language are coextensive, for Saussure.

Saussure's real importance for French structuralism and post-structuralism, however, lies less in his largely implicit account of how language relates to the mind and to the world than in his highly explicit account of how the elements of language relate to each other. First of all, "the link between signifier and signified is arbitrary." Indeed, since the linguistic sign is itself a signifier joined to a signified, it suffices to say that "*the linguistic sign is arbitrary.*"[10] However, this "must not be taken to imply that a signifier depends on the free choice of the speaker."[11] Rather, it means that there is no necessary link between the concept *tree* and the sound that English speakers use to represent it. "The same idea might as well be represented by any other sequence of sounds," as is demonstrated "by the existence of different languages."[12] *Tree, arbre, Baum, dendron, 'ets, crann*—in principle the chain is endless. "No one disputes the fact that linguistic signs are arbitrary," admits Saussure,[13] "[b]ut it is often easier to discover a

8. Ibid., 9, italics removed; cf. 230. By bracketing the referential function of language, Saussure (inadvertently?) moves in the direction of one form of philosophical skepticism: the external world exists but it cannot be known as such. For a more precise characterization of Saussure's philosophical location, see Berman, *From the New Criticism to Deconstruction*, 115–19.

9. Saussure, *Course in General Linguistics*, 110.

10. Ibid., 67, his emphasis.

11. Ibid., 68.

12. Ibid., 67–68.

13. Although he does proceed meticulously to deal with two apparent exceptions to the rule, namely, onomatopoeia and exclamations. He

truth than to assign it to its correct place," he adds, implying that the real consequences of this uncontroversial assertion have never been properly grasped.[14] Indeed, the principle of arbitrariness "is the organizing principle for the whole of linguistics," for Saussure, and "the consequences which flow from this principle are innumerable."[15]

The most important of these consequences for French structuralism, and above all for poststructuralism, was this: What is not arbitrary about the signifier, but necessary in order that it have meaning, are the *differences* that distinguish it from all the other signifiers in the linguistic system. The sound *tree*, for example, is intelligible to an English speaker not because of what it *is*, strictly speaking, since there is no resemblance between the sound (or its appearance when written) and the concept of a tree, much less the actual physical object that goes by that name. Instead, the sound is intelligible precisely because of what it *is not*, which is to say *three, thee, the, tea*, and every other sound in the English language. As Saussure puts it, "two signs *a* and *b* are never grasped as such by our linguistic consciousness, but only the difference between *a* and *b*."[16] In short, meaning is the product of difference, and Saussure goes on to make his famous claim: "*In the language itself, there are only differences.* Even more important than that is the fact that, although in general a difference presupposes positive terms between which the difference holds, in a language there are only differences, *and no positive terms.*"[17]

Alarmed at his own audacity, Saussure then backs away from the brink to which he has brought us: "But to say that in a language everything is negative holds only for signified and signifier considered separately. The moment we consider the sign as a whole, we encounter something which is positive in its own domain. . . . Although signified and signifier are each, in isolation, purely differential and negative, their combination is in fact of a positive nature."[18] Indeed, "the moment

argues that neither violates the rule of arbitrariness. In the case of onomatopoeia, for example, one can distinguish the French dog's *ouaoua* from the German dog's *wauwau* and the English dog's *woof woof* or *bowwow* (ibid., 69).

14. Ibid., 68.
15. Ibid.
16. Ibid., 116.
17. Ibid., 118, his emphasis.
18. Ibid., 118–19.

we compare one sign with another as positive combination," he continues, now in full retreat, "the term *difference* should be dropped. It is no longer appropriate."[19] Note the contradiction: although the (arbitrary) signifier's bond with its signified does not prevent the resulting sign from being arbitrary—"the linguistic sign is arbitrary"[20]—their fusion does somehow prevent the sign from being a radically differential and essentially negative entity, notwithstanding the fact that "the terms *arbitrary* and *differential* designate two correlative properties."[21]

DECONSTRUCTING METAPHYSICS (AND DISABUSING ONESELF OF THE NOTION THAT IT CAN BE DONE)

In a series of texts dating from the late 1960s, Derrida began to think Saussure's unfinished thoughts for him. Earlier we noted a problem with Saussure's definition of the signified, his term for "concept." Given that the signifier (or "sound pattern") is already sound as mentally processed—"the hearer's psychological impression of a sound"[22]—it sounds itself suspiciously like a concept. The question then arises as to whether the sign's *official* conceptual component, the signified, is left with any real work to do.[23]

Derrida applies Ockham's razor to Saussure's two-faced sign, questioning Saussure's "maintenance of the rigorous distinction between signifier and signified."[24] Derrida suspects that the careful maintenance of this distinction masks a metaphysical and theological investment, since it "inherently leaves open the possibility of thinking a *concept signified in and of itself*, a concept simply present for thought, independent of a relationship to . . . a system of signifiers."[25] Derrida's term for such a concept is a *transcendental signified*, "which in and of itself, in its essence, would refer to no signifier, would exceed the

---

19. Ibid., 119.
20. Ibid., 67.
21. Ibid., 116.
22. Ibid., 66.
23. Cf. Berman, *From the New Criticism to Deconstruction*, 116.
24. Jacques Derrida, *Positions*, trans. Alan Bass (Chicago: University of Chicago Press, 1981), 19.
25. Ibid., his emphasis.

chain of signs, and would no longer itself function as a signifier."[26] For Derrida, the entire history of Western thought bespeaks the "powerful, systematic, and irrepressible desire" for such a signified, an order of being that would be fundamental and immutable, and "place a reassuring end to the reference from sign to sign."[27]

For Derrida, moreover, the transcendental signified, in all its guises and disguises, has always had a special relationship to *presence*. In "Structure, Sign, and Play" he claims "that all the names related to fundamentals . . . have always designated an invariable presence." A list then follows, largely made up of Greek terms with a philosophical or theological resonance—"*eidos* [Platonic essence], *arche* [beginning, origin, founding principle], *telos* [end, final goal, closure], *energeia* [energy, Aristotelian completion], *ousia* [which Derrida himself glosses as 'essence, existence, substance, subject'], *aletheia* [truth], transcendentality, consciousness, God, man, and so forth."[28] A similar list occurs in *Of Grammatology*; again the issue is "the historical determination of the meaning of being in general as *presence*"—"presence of the thing to the sight as *eidos*, presence as substance/essence/existence (*ousia*), temporal presence as point (*stigme*) of the now or of the moment (*nun*), the self-presence of the cogito, consciousness, subjectivity, the co-presence of the other and of the self . . . and so forth."[29]

Saussure provides Derrida with a theory of language that enables him to contest this "historical determination" of being as presence. Derridean deconstruction is in part a kind of super-Saussureanism, an emphatic affirmation of Saussure's seminal insight that language is a system of differences "without positive terms," joined to an equally emphatic rejection of Saussure's order of signifieds—a rejection based on the *Cours* itself. For Saussure seems to have realized that signifieds, no less than signifiers, can only be grasped differentially and relationally, through their differences from other signifieds, other concepts. "Concepts . . . are purely differential," he conceded; "that is to say they are concepts defined not positively, in terms of their content, but negatively by contrast with other items in the same system. What characterizes each most exactly is being whatever the others are

26. Ibid., 19–20.
27. Derrida, *Of Grammatology*, 49.
28. Derrida, "Structure, Sign, and Play," 279–80.
29. Derrida, *Of Grammatology*, 12.

not."[30] But Saussure hesitated to draw what, for Derrida, is the obvious conclusion, namely, that the very distinction between signifier and signified is itself an arbitrary one, since "the signified always already functions as a signifier."[31] For Derrida, this "apparently innocent proposition"[32] has far-reaching consequences. As he puts it in "Structure, Sign, and Play," an essay that everywhere presupposes Saussure while never bothering to mention him by name, "This was the moment when language invaded the universal problematic, the moment when, in the absence of a center or origin, everything became discourse . . . , a system in which the central signified, the original or transcendental signified, is never absolutely present outside a system of differences. The absence of the transcendental signified extends the domain and the play of signification infinitely."[33]

To summarize what I have been saying thus far, Derrida has metaphysics for his target ("metaphysics" being Derridean shorthand for "any science of presence"),[34] and one of his principal weapons is Saussure's innocuous-sounding claim that language is a system of differences without positive terms. For what this play of differences prevents is any single element in a language, or any other sign system for that matter,[35] from being simply present in and of itself. Each element is able to signify only because of its relationship to something that it is not, from which it differs, and which itself cannot simply be present, but is in turn a mere effect of the traces within it of all the other elements in the system—"infinite implication," in other words.[36] "Nothing, neither among the elements nor within the system, is anywhere ever simply present or absent. There are only, everywhere, differences and traces of traces."[37] Or to put it yet another way,

30. Saussure, *Course in General Linguistics*, 115.
31. Derrida, *Of Grammatology*, 7.
32. Ibid., 73.
33. Derrida, "Structure, Sign, and Play," 280.
34. Gayatri Chakravorty Spivak, "Translator's Preface," in Derrida, *Of Grammatology*, xxi.
35. Derrida's conception of intertextuality, for example, can be gleaned by substituting the word "text" for the word "element" in the ensuing sentences. His most explicit statement on intertextuality occurs in "Living On: Border Lines," trans. James Hulbert, in Harold Bloom et al., *Deconstruction and Criticism* (New York: Continuum, 1979), 83–84.
36. Cf. Jacques Derrida, "Force and Signification," in *Writing and Difference*, 25.
37. Derrida, *Positions*, 26.

the movement of signification is possible only if each so-called "pres-ent" element, each element appearing on the scene of presence, is related to something other than itself, thereby keeping within itself the mark of the past element, and already letting itself be vitiated by the mark of its relation to the future element, this trace . . . constituting what is called the present by means of this very relation to what it is not: what it absolutely is not, not even a past or a future as a modified present. An interval must separate the present from what it is not in order for the present to be itself, but this interval that constitutes it as present must, by the same token, divide the present in and of itself, thereby also dividing, along with the present, every-thing that is thought on the basis of the present[38]

—which is to say, God, being, essence, identity, consciousness, self, intentionality, meaning, and so on. "Difference is what enables mean-ing," said Saussure. In effect, Derrida finishes the sentence for him: "Then meaning is present, and presence itself can mean what it *has* meant for Western metaphysics, only as an effect of difference."

Yet metaphysics is not so easily dispatched. "There is no sense in doing without the concepts of metaphysics in order to shake met-aphysics," admits Derrida. "We have no language—no syntax and no lexicon—which is foreign to this history; we can pronounce not a single deconstructive proposition which has not already had to slip into the form, the logic, and the implicit postulations of precisely what it seeks to contest."[39] Even in the case of Saussure's two-story sign, for example, the fact that the opposition between the signifier and the signified cannot be absolute, or even radical, "does not prevent it from functioning, and even from being indispensable within certain limits—very wide limits."[40] The overcoming or end of metaphysics cannot even be envisioned, much less brought about, any more than can a reality without origin or end, foundations or center, presence, hierarchy, iden-tity, meaning, existence—all metaphysical concepts. Derrida's decon-struction of metaphysics can be undertaken only from within the edifice that metaphysics provides—a project requiring vigilance, stealth, and extreme cunning.

38. Jacques Derrida, "Différance," in *Margins of Philosophy*, trans. Alan Bass (Chicago: University of Chicago Press, 1982), 13.
39. Derrida, "Structure, Sign, and Play," 280–81.
40. Derrida, *Positions*, 20.

CAN NEGATIVE THEOLOGY MAKE A *DIFFÉRANCE?*

Nowhere is this vigilance more evident than in "La Différance," a lecture Derrida delivered at the Sorbonne in 1968. There he points out that that which produces presence cannot itself be reduced to presence; or as he himself puts it, "what makes possible the presentation of the being-present" can never be "presented as such" or "offered to the present. Or to anyone."[41] Not even to Derrida, then, although that will not deter him from pretending not to look for it, or from giving it a name, *différance.*

Like so many of Derrida's essays, "La Différance" is exquisitely subtle and cautious, which is also to say, exceedingly slow and ponderous. The word *différance* is a neologism, French *différence* spelled with an *a*. Why spell it with an *a*? After five pages of preliminary "precautions," Derrida decides to "attempt a simple and approximate semantic analysis that will take us to within sight of what is at stake" in this misspelling.[42] His analysis is far from simple, in fact, but here is what it comes down to. The French verb *différer* "has two meanings which seem quite distinct."[43] On the one hand, it means "to defer" and all that that entails—delay, detour, and so on. This would be the *temporal* trajectory of the verb. On the other hand, and indeed more commonly, *différer* means "to differ," and since differing requires a modicum of distance between elements, this would be the *spatial* trajectory of the verb. (These two trajectories cannot keep their hands off each other, as it turns out. The word "interval" would be symptomatic of this attraction, since it has both a temporal and a spatial aspect.) The word *différance*, therefore, is suspended between differing and deferring, "the becoming-time of space and the becoming-space of time."[44] *Différance* is also, or especially, Saussurean *différence* writ large.[45]

This unwieldy neologism is given a prodigious amount of delicate work to do in Derrida's dense essay. *Différance* is patiently honed and refined until it becomes sufficiently subtle and strong to slip into

41. Derrida, "Différance," 6.
42. Ibid., 7.
43. Ibid.
44. Ibid., 8.
45. Cf. ibid., 10–12, 15.

the hairline cracks in the prison walls, to test "the limit which has always constrained us, which still constrains us—as inhabitants of a language and a system of thought—to formulate the meaning of Being in general as presence or absence."[46]

To begin with, if presence, being, essence, identity, center, origin, end, and all the rest are mere effects of difference—or better, of *différance*—then *différance* itself cannot be reduced to any of these qualities or categories. "Already we have had to delineate *that différance is not*, does not exist, is not a present-being . . . in any form; and we will be led to delineate also everything that it *is not*, that is, *everything*; and consequently that it has neither existence nor essence. It derives from no category of being, whether present or absent."[47] As such, *différance* is "irreducible to any ontological or theological . . . reappropriation," because "as the very opening of the space" in which ontology and theology become possible, it includes them and simultaneously exceeds them.[48] Something like an "originary *différance*" begins to come into view, therefore—although it cannot properly be termed "orginary," for the concept of the origin has always denoted a presence of some sort or other, and *différance* is irreducible to presence, or, for that matter, to "its simple symmetrical opposite, absence or lack."[49] (Deconstruction is not a philosophy of absence, then, any more than it is a philosophy of presence, since absence too is an effect of *différance*.)

By the same token, *différance* cannot be regarded as simply another philosophical concept, however subtle, since it is "the possibility of conceptuality" in general.[50] Differences are what make concepts possible, as we have seen. But "this does not mean that the *différance* that produces differences is somehow before them, in a simple and unmodified—in-different—present. *Différance* is the nonfull, non-simple, structured and differentiating origin of differences." Thus, once again, "the name 'origin' no longer suits it."[51]

Derrida returns to the problem of the origin a little later: "Differences . . . are 'produced'—deferred—by *différance*. But *what*

46. Ibid., 10.
47. Ibid., 6.
48. Ibid.
49. Ibid., 10.
50. Ibid., 11.
51. Ibid.

defers or *who* defers?"[52] To ask such questions, however, is to risk falling back "into what we have just disengaged ourselves from."[53] In particular, we must not surrender to the belief that *différance* "is to be mastered and governed on the basis of the point of a present being, which itself could be some thing, a form, a state, a power in the world to which all kinds of names might be given, a *what*, or a present being as a *subject*, a *who*."[54] It is not difficult to guess who this "who" might be.

In the lively discussion that followed the original presentation of "La Différance," one participant was audacious or innocent enough to remark: "[This *différance*] is the source of everything and one cannot know it: it is the God of negative theology."[55] Possibly he had wandered in late or, more likely, had fallen asleep. Several pages into his paper, Derrida had said of *différance*: "Reserving itself, not exposing itself, in regular fashion it exceeds the order of truth at a certain precise point"—"truth" as a form of presence, that is—"but without dissimulating itself as something, as a mysterious being, in the occult of a nonknowledge."[56] In other words, "Don't take me for a theologian, although I'll be displaying several of the symptoms." In particular, "the detours, locutions, and syntax" in which Derrida "will often have to take recourse will resemble those of negative theology, occasionally even to the point of being indistinguishable from negative theology."[57] The reader is quickly reassured, however, that those aspects of *différance* that Derrida will delineate through negation—not this, not that— "are not theological, not even in the order of the most negative of negative theologies."[58]

What is negative theology? For most religion scholars, the term readily conjures up an esoteric tradition of mystical speculation associated with such names as Pseudo-Dionysius and Meister Eckhart, although the concept of negative theology can also be expanded to take in elements of a more diverse range of thinkers—Plato, Philo,

52. Ibid., 14.
53. Ibid.
54. Ibid., 15; cf. 21–22.
55. "The Original Discussion of 'Différance,' " trans. David Wood, Sarah Richmond, and Malcolm Bernard, in *Derrida and* Différance, 84.
56. Ibid., 6.
57. Ibid.
58. Ibid.

Origen, Gregory of Nyssa, Augustine, even Wittgenstein. Crudely put, what these wildly disparate writers share in common is a conviction that human thought and language are inadequate to comprehend the divine. In consequence, negative theology can be said to be a self-subverting discourse that systematically showcases its own inadequacy to the theological task of enclosing God in concepts—a stuttering disruption of the confident assertions of conventional theological discourse. In short, negative theology is the deconstruction of positive theology.[59]

Différance should not be confused with the ineffable God of negative theology, however, or so Derrida assures us: "This unnameable"—*différance*—"is not an ineffable Being which no name could approach: God, for example."[60] He reiterated the point in the discussion that followed his lecture: "*Différance* is not, it is not a being and it is not God (if, that is, this name is given to a being, even a supreme being)."[61] This is why his own discourse, despite its "resemblances" to negative theology, is ultimately "alien to negative theology."[62] And yet Derrida himself has never tired of demonstrating that the alien is always already within, that the two poles in any binary opposition (here, negative theology vs. Derridean philosophy) are always already implicated in each other in ways that complicate the opposition. Thus it is not surprising that he adds: "And yet, as often happens, this infinite distance [between negative theology and his own philosophy] is also an infinitesimal distance. That is why negative theology fascinates me."[63] And that, too, is why he has never ceased not to write on it, writing something altogether different, altogether *différant*, infinitely

59. Cf. Kevin Hart, *The Trespass of the Sign: Deconstruction, Theology and Philosophy* (New York: Cambridge University Press, 1989), 202. This deconstruction is accomplished within the confines of positive theology. Michel Despland advises: "Let us clearly set aside vizualizations of large territories demarcated and occupied by 'positive' theologies, contrasted with smaller but firmer grounds held by 'negative' theologies. Neither should negative theologies be viewed as the 'opposite' of the positive ones. They are rather moments of them, correctives one might perhaps say" ("On Not Solving Riddles Alone," in *Derrida and Negative Theology*, ed. Harold Coward and Toby Foshay [Albany: SUNY Press, 1992], 147).
60. Derrida, "Différance," 26.
61. "The Original Discussion of 'Différance,' " 85.
62. Ibid.
63. Ibid. Compare the epigraph to the present chapter.

yet infinitesimally *différant*. To put it another way, Derrida has never ceased to write on *différance*, and this writing has always had an intimate relationship to negative theology.

Derrida has never ceased to write on *différance* to the extent that *différance* itself is but a single link in an open chain of "nonterms." "*[D]ifférance* lends itself to a certain number of nonsynonymous substitutions, according to the necessity of the context," he explains[64]— "nonsynonymous" because of the "impossibility" of the synonym, a term that points outwards and upwards toward a transcendental signified, as do "translation," "summary," "definition," and other such terms. Each conjures up the illusion of an essential, pure, transposable meaning capable of manifesting itself in different linguistic incarnations.[65] (Thus Derrida will insist that to say "deconstruction is X" is precisely to miss the point.)[66]

The contexts that determine the various transformations of *différance*, its mutation into "a certain number of nonsynonymous substitutions," are, for the most part, specific texts: Derrida's writings are almost all readings of other writings, philosophical or literary, and as he reads he likes to lift individual words from these texts and give them a strategic role. These are the "nonsynonymous subsitutions" for *différance*. They include such terms as *pharmakon* from Plato's *Phaedrus*, *supplement* from certain works by the French philosopher Jean-Jacques Rousseau, and *hymen* from a prose poem by the French modernist writer Stéphane Mallarmé. Each of these three terms has a special relationship to writing, as we shall see. Indeed, in order to begin to grasp the slippery chain of "nonterms" in which *différance* is enmeshed, we must first grasp the significance of writing, and also of speech, in Derrida's own writings.

"THE GARDEN IS SPEECH, THE DESERT WRITING"

As Derrida sees it, Western thought has almost always based itself on binary oppositions. Occasionally, he hazards a brief list of some of the more important of these oppositions.[67] A more ample list might read

64. Derrida, "Différance," 12.
65. Cf. Derrida, *Positions*, 20.
66. Derrida, "Letter to a Japanese Friend," 4.
67. See, e.g, Derrida, *Positions* 29, 43, and "Différance," 17.

as follows: transcendent/immanent, intelligible/sensible, spirit (mind, soul)/body, presence/absence, necessary/contingent, essence/accident, primary/secondary, nature/culture, masculine/feminine, white/black (brown, red, yellow), heterosexual/homosexual, normal/abnormal, sane/insane, conscious/unconscious, identity/difference, positive/negative, inside/outside, central/marginal, object/representation, objective/subjective, history/fiction, serious/trivial, literal/metaphorical, content/form, signified/signifier, original/copy, speech/writing, text/interpretation, text/context, primary text/secondary text, and so on. For Derrida, binary thinking is necessarily oppressive: "In a classical philosophical opposition we are not dealing with the peaceful coexistence of a vis-à-vis but rather with a violent hierarchy. One of the two terms governs the other . . . or has the upper hand."[68] Thus, the first term in each of the pairs above is privileged at the expense of the second term.

Derrida is not alone in his suspicion. Across the entire spectrum of academic disciplines, ever-increasing numbers of scholars seem intent on subverting hierarchical oppositions, certain oppositions in particular: male/female, masculine/feminine, white/nonwhite, and—in recent literary and cultural studies—heterosexual/homosexual. Deconstruction has undoubtedly been a catalyst in this development. Naomi Schor notes, for example, that

> the intersection of feminism and deconstruction has been the site of some of the most productive and irreconcilable critical exchanges in the 1980s. One primary reason has been the use of deconstruction to critique "essentialism" as a "ruse of metaphysics." This association of deconstruction and antiessentialism has led some materialist feminists to enlist deconstruction in their battle against ahistorical essences such as "woman." Others . . . resist it, suspecting Derridean antiessentialism as being a ruse of patriarchy, all the while recognizing in deconstruction a powerful lever for unsettling the paradigm of sexual difference and valorizing the previously devalorized term.[69]

Derrida himself has attempted to come to grips with the issues raised by feminists,[70] and he has also written on racial oppression in

68. Derrida, *Positions*, 41.
69. Schor, "Feminist and Gender Studies," 272–73.
70. See, e.g., Jacques Derrida, *Spurs: Nietzsche's Styles/Éperons: Les Styles de Nietzsche*, trans. Barbara Harlow (Chicago: University of Chicago

South Africa.[71] These late supplements to his oeuvre are not harnessed nearly as often by feminists and other politically minded critics, however, as his better-known early works—*Of Grammatology* and *Writing and Difference* (both dating from 1967, along with the less-often-read *Speech and Phenomena*), as well as *Positions, Margins of Philosophy*, and *Dissemination* (all three dating from 1972).[72] As it happens, these early writings and interviews tend to focus on one opposition more than any other—not the oppositions of gender, race, or class, however, but an opposition that at first glance seems inconsequential by comparison, that of speech vs. writing.

Of course, the relationship between speech and writing, Word and Book, is also an issue for Christianity. Walter J. Ong puts it nicely:

> In Christian teaching orality-literacy polarities are particularly acute, probably more acute than in any other religious tradition, even the Hebrew. For in Christian teaching the Second Person of the One Godhead, who redeemed mankind from sin, is known not only as the Son but also as the Word of God. In this teaching, God the Father utters or speaks His Word, his Son. He does not inscribe him. The very Person of the Son is constituted as the Word of the Father. Yet Christian teaching also presents at its core the written word of God, the Bible, which, back of its human authors, has God as author as no other writing does. In what way are the two senses of God's "word" related to one another and to human beings in history?[73]

Press, 1979); "Interview: Choreographies," in Jacques Derrida, *The Ear of the Other: Otobiography, Transference, Translation*, ed. Christie McDonald, trans. Avital Ronell and Peggy Kamuf (Lincoln: University of Nebraska Press, 1985), 163–85; "Women in the Beehive: A Seminar with Jacques Derrida," in *Men in Feminism*, ed. Alice Jardine and Paul Smith (New York: Methuen, 1987), 189–203.

71. See, e.g., Jacques Derrida, "Racism's Last Word," trans. Peggy Kamuf, in *"Race," Writing and Difference*, ed. Henry Louis Gates, Jr. (Chicago: University of Chicago Press, 1986), 329–38; idem, "But, beyond . . . (Open Letter to Anne McClintock and Rob Nixon)," trans. Peggy Kamuf, *Critical Inquiry* 13 (1986): 140–54; *For Nelson Mandela*, ed. Jacques Derrida and Mustapha Tlili (New York: Seaver Books, 1987).

72. Gayatri Spivak complains: "The early Derrida can certainly be shown to be useful for feminist practice, but why is it that, when he writes under the sign of woman, as it were, his work becomes solipsistic and marginal?" (*In Other Worlds: Essays in Cultural Politics* [New York: Routledge, 1988], 84; cf. 91).

73. Walter J. Ong, *Orality and Literacy: The Technologizing of the Word* (New York: Methuen, 1982), 179.

Although Derrida has written around the Bible on occasion,[74] he has never directly tackled the relationship of speech and writing in the biblical texts, or in the Jewish or Christian theological traditions generally.[75] His hypothesis—part argument, part assertion, as we shall see—is that throughout Western history, speech has almost always been idealized at the expense of writing, writing being denigrated by comparison, considered a necessary evil, if not evil or corrupt altogether. And he singles out Plato, Rousseau, Hegel, Saussure, and Husserl as exemplars of this tendency, "specific nuclei in a process and a system."[76]

But what could be more natural than so to privilege speech? "I would rather not use paper and ink; instead I hope to come to you and talk with you face to face, so that our joy may be complete," writes the Johannine elder to his "elect lady" (2 John 12). As I speak, my words appear to be one with my thoughts. My meaning appears to be fully present both to me and to my hearer, provided I am speaking effectively, affectively. "My words are 'alive' because they seem not to leave me: not to fall outside me, outside my breath, at a visible distance; not to cease to belong to me."[77] At such moments, the voice, the breath, appear to be consciousness itself, presence itself.

Voice, presence, truth. As we have already seen, Derrida claims that all the names used to designate theological or philosophical fundamentals in the West have always designated "the constant of a presence": God, being, essence, existence, substance, subject, object, consciousness, and so on. Derrida's phrase for this litany of names, and

74. See Further Reading for examples. Additional examples are listed in Moore, *Mark and Luke in Poststructuralist Perspectives,* xv n. 7.

75. He comes closest in "Edmond Jabès and the Question of the Book," in *Writing and Difference,* 64–78.

76. Jacques Derrida, "The Pit and the Pyramid: Introduction to Hegel's Semiology," in *Margins of Philosophy,* 94. For Derrida's most sustained reading of Plato in this regard, see "Plato's Pharmacy," in *Dissemination,* trans. Barbara Johnson (Chicago: University of Chicago Press, 1981), 61–171; for Rousseau (discussed with Lévi-Strauss), see *Of Grammatology,* 97–316; for Hegel, see "Outwork, Prefacing," in *Dissemination,* 1–59, "The Pit and the Pyramid," and *Glas;* for Saussure, see *Of Grammatology,* 27–73, and *Positions,* 17–36; and for Husserl, see *Speech and Phenomena and Other Essays on Husserl's Theory of Signs,* trans. David B. Allison (Evanston, Ill.: Northwestern University Press, 1973), and *Edmund Husserl's* Origin of Geometry: *An Introduction,* trans. John P. Leavey, Jr. (Stony Brook, N.Y.: Nicholas Hays, 1978).

77. Derrida, *Speech and Phenomena,* 76.

all it entails, is *the metaphysics of presence.* He claims, moreover, that in mainstream Western thought, speech has always been the paradigm not only for every form of presence but also for every form of truth.[78] ("In the beginning was the Word [*logos*], and the Word was with God, and the Word was God.") Derrida uses another term, *logocentrism,* to denote the special relationship of the *logos* (speech, logic, reason, Word of God) and the idea of presence. "[L]ogocentrism is an ethnocentric metaphysics. It is related to the history of the West."[79]

That history, or the version of it that won out, began in a garden ("They heard the sound of the Lord God walking in the garden at the time of the evening breeze, and the man and his wife hid themselves from the presence of the Lord God" [Gen. 3:8]). "The garden is speech," declared the Jewish poet Edmond Jabès.[80] Derrida extends Jabès's allegory: "God no longer speaks to us; he has interrupted himself: we must take words upon ourselves. We must . . . entrust ourselves to traces . . . because we have ceased hearing the voice from within the immediate proximity of the garden. . . . The *difference* between speech and writing is sin, . . . lost immediacy, work outside the garden."[81] Outside the garden there is only sand and separation: "Writing is the moment of the desert as the moment of Separation."[82] Writing begins "with the stifling of [the] voice and the dissimulation of [the] Face," which are first of all the voice and face of God.[83] Writing defaces every theology of presence.

As lifeless written marks in place of present living speech, writing has often seemed to be an inferior, if necessary, substitute for speech. Cut off from the *pneuma* (spirit or breath), severed at its source from the authorizing presence of a speaker, writing has often been thought to threaten truth with distortion and mischief. Plato has Socrates say, "Once a thing is put into writing, the composition . . . drifts all over the place, getting into the hands not only of those who understand it, but equally of those who have no business with it; it doesn't know how to address the right people, and not address the

78. Derrida, *Of Grammatology,* 20.
79. Ibid., 79.
80. Edmond Jabès, *Le Livre des questions* (Paris: Gallimard, 1963), 169, quoted in Derrida, "Edmond Jabès and the Question of the Book," 68.
81. Derrida, "Edmond Jabès and the Question of the Book," 68.
82. Ibid.
83. Ibid., 67.

wrong. And when it is ill-treated and unfairly abused it always needs its parent to come to its help."[84] An orphan and a delinquent, no sooner born than set adrift, cut loose from the author who gave birth to it, writing seems fated endlessly to circulate, if not from foster home to foster home, then from reader to reader, the best of whom can never be sure that he or she has fully grasped what the author intended to say. For authors have a way of being absent, even dead, and their intended meaning can no longer be directly intuited, or double-checked through question and answer, as in the face-to-face situation of speech. Hence Derrida's hyperbole: "I hardly have the time to sign than I am already dead . . . because the structure of the 'signature' event carries my death in that event."[85] But it is not only the author who is dead. It is a property of writing always to be able to readdress itself to readers that its author could never have foreseen, which is to say that "the possibility of the 'death' of the [intended] addressee is inscribed in the structure of the written mark."[86] Hence a second hyperbole: "If I say that I write for dead addressees, not dead in the future but already dead at the moment when I get to the end of a sentence, it is not in order to play."[87]

Derrida deconstructs the opposition of speech and writing. ("The crack between the two is nothing. The crack is what one must occupy.")[88] But to deconstruct a hierarchical opposition is not simply to argue that the term ordinarily repressed is in reality the superior term. Rather than stand the opposition on its head in front of a mirror, thereby inverting it but leaving it intact nonetheless, deconstruction attempts to show how each term in the opposition is joined to its companion by an intricate network of arteries. In consequence, the line ordinarily drawn between the two terms is shown to be a political and not a natural reality. "Like Czechoslovakia and

84. Plato, *Phaedrus*, in *The Collected Dialogues of Plato*, ed. Edith Hamilton and Huntington Cairns, trans. R. Hackforth (Princeton, N.J.: Princeton University Press, 1961), 275d–e. Derrida discusses this passage in "Plato's Pharmacy," 77, and "Signature Event Context," in *Margins of Philosophy*, 316.

85. Derrida, *Glas*, 19b.

86. Derrida, "Signature Event Context," 316.

87. Jacques Derrida, "Envois," in *The Post Card: From Socrates to Freud and Beyond*, trans. Alan Bass (Chicago: University of Chicago Press, 1987), 33.

88. Derrida, *Glas*, 207b.

Poland, [they] resemble each other, regard each other, separated none-theless by a frontier all the more mysterious . . . because it is abstract, legal, ideal."[89] But as such it can always be redrawn. Derrida approaches the border between speech and writing by asking, in effect: What if the illegal alien, the parasite, were already within? What if speech were already the host of writing? What if the immediacy of speech, the sensation of presence it produces, were but a mirage?

This brings us back to Derrida's deployment of Saussure. For Saussure, as we saw, language is a system of differences "without positive terms." And for Derrida, what this play of differences prevents is any single element in language simply being present in and of itself. Each element is able to signify only through a relationship to something that it is not, and which itself cannot simply be present, but whose meaning is in turn an effect of the traces within it of all the other elements in language. In consequence, for Derrida, nothing is ever simply present or absent. The present is irremediably divided from itself, and with it every metaphysical concept with an investment in the idea of presence: God, being, essence, identity, consciousness, self, intentionality, and so on. Now, Derrida terms this uncontrollable spill-age *writing* (*l'écriture*)—not writing as ordinarily conceived, however, which is to say as a substitute or storage container for speech, but a generalized writing, a writing writ large. This is what it means to say that speech is already the host of writing: "Discontinuity, delay, het-erogeneity, and alterity already were working upon the voice, producing it from its first breath as a system of differential traces, that is as writing before the letter."[90]

The disseminating flow of this general writing swirls and ed-dies through the spoken word with unsensed and unsuspected force, eroding the apparently simple, intuitive self-identity of even the most immediate-seeming speech event. And this, for Derrida, is why writing in the restricted sense has always been suspect in the West, why the crime of Cain has so often been attributed to it: "[O]ne realizes that what was chased off limits, the wandering outcast . . . has indeed never ceased to haunt language as its primary and most intimate possibility."[91]

89. Ibid., 189b.
90. Derrida, "Qual Quelle: Valéry's Sources," in *Margins of Philosophy*, 291.
91. Derrida, *Of Grammatology*, 44.

But *has* writing always been suspect throughout Western history—"from Plato to Rousseau," as Derrida likes to say? From Plato to Rousseau is a gulf of some two thousand years, but one that Derrida takes a running jump at time and time again. For example: "One can follow the treatment accorded to writing . . . from Plato to Rousseau, Saussure, Husserl, occasionally Heidegger himself."[92] Or again: "[T]his was also Plato's gesture and Rousseau's, as it will also be Saussure's."[93] Or even: "[N]ot only from Plato to Hegel . . . but also, beyond these apparent limits, from the pre-Socratics to Heidegger, . . . the history of truth . . . has always been—except for a metaphysical diversion that we shall have to explain—the debasement of writing, and its repression outside 'full' speech."[94] The sole stop-off point between Plato and Rousseau is Aristotle, a small outcrop on the edge of the abyss: "[F]rom Plato to Husserl, passing through Aristotle, Rousseau, Hegel, etc."[95]

Does Derrida really alight safely on Rousseau, or does he splatter on the far wall of the canyon long before reaching him? In other words, does the suspicion of writing evident in Plato's *Phaedrus* extend, more or less uniformly, through the many centuries that separate him from Rousseau and other Enlightenment and post-Enlightenment figures? Here we turn again to Walter Ong. Having contented himself with passing swipes at Derrida in his previous books, Ong finally locks horns with him in *Orality and Literacy*. Ong criticizes Derrida and deconstruction on a number of counts. Drawing on the work of Eric Havelock, for example, Ong argues that Plato's attitude toward writing was more ambivalent than Derrida allows.[96] Significantly, however, Ong does not contest the Derridean generalization "from Plato to Saussure"; on the contrary, he implicitly lends support to it. "Long after a culture has begun to use writing, it may still not give writing high ratings," writes Ong. "A present-day literate usually assumes that written records have more force than spoken words," whereas "earlier cultures that knew literacy but had not so fully interiorized it, have often assumed quite the opposite."[97] Later Ong argues that

92. Derrida, *Positions*, 7.
93. Derrida, "The Pit and the Pyramid," 94.
94. Derrida, *Of Grammatology*, 3.
95. Derrida, *Positions*, 22.
96. Ong, *Orality and Literacy*, 167–68; cf. 80–81.
97. Ibid., 96.

manuscript culture in the west remained always marginally oral. Ambrose of Milan caught the earlier mood in his *Commentary on Luke* (iv. 5): "Sight is often deceived, hearing serves as guarantee." In the west through the Renaissance, the oration was the most taught of all verbal productions and remained implicitly the basic paradigm for all discourse, written as well as oral. Written material was subsidiary to hearing in ways which strike us today as bizarre. Writing served largely to recycle knowledge back into the oral world, as in medieval university disputations, in the reading of literary and other texts to groups . . . , and in reading aloud even when reading to oneself. At least as late as the twelfth century in England, checking even written financial accounts was still done aurally, by having them read aloud.[98]

Also in medieval England, oral testimony was judged prima facie to be more credible than written testimony: unlike living witnesses, texts were incapable of responding to questions, of clarifying and defending their statements—exactly one of Plato's objections to writing.[99] The subsequent introduction of print in Europe, moreover, elicited misgivings in certain quarters that clearly echoed Plato's misgivings concerning writing. For example, "Hieronimo Squarciafico, who in fact promoted the printing of the Latin classics, also argued in 1477 that already 'abundance of books makes men less studious': it destroys memory and enfeebles the mind by relieving it of too much work."[100]

An earlier book of Ong's, *Interfaces of the Word*, lends further support to Derrida's hypothesis. Ong makes much of the perennial association of writing with death, the most famous example being 2 Cor. 3:6—"the letter kills, but the Spirit gives life"—although the same association is also implicit in Plato's arguments and explicit in "countless other texts . . . from secular and religious sources."[101] Notable among such texts is Luther's elaboration of Paul: "[Moses'] pen is a dead and hollow reed. . . . But the tongue is solid and full flesh, and it produces living letters in the heart, with words that have been poured

98. Ibid., 119.

99. Ibid., 96.

100. Ibid., 80.

101. Walter J. Ong, *Interfaces of the Word: Studies in the Evolution of Consciousness and Culture* (Ithaca, N.Y.: Cornell University Press, 1977), 237. He lists numerous examples, ranging from ancient to modern writers (236–38).

in through the ear. . . . Therefore the church does not acknowledge letters, nor the reed which draws them, but it acknowledges the spoken words which the tongue, or tongues of fire produce."[102] Among these phobic statements too, ironically, is the following one from Ong himself: "Though serviceable and enriching beyond all measure, nevertheless, by comparision with the oral medium, writing and print are permanently decadent."[103] And again: "All reductions of the spoken word to nonauditory media, however necessary they may be, attenuate and debase it, as Plato so intensely felt."[104]

In would appear, therefore, that there is at least a rope bridge linking Plato's statements on writing with those of Rousseau and his successors. But to begin to clamber out on that bridge might be to risk missing one's step, or at any rate to miss the point. For according to Paul de Man, one of Derrida's more astute readers, Derrida is merely "telling a story." Throughout *Of Grammatology*, claims de Man, "Derrida uses Heidegger's and Nietzsche's fiction of metaphysics as a *period* in Western thought in order to dramatize, to give tension and suspense to the argument. . . . Neither is Derrida taken in by the theatricality of his gesture or the fiction of his narrative."[105]

This is a matter of opinion, however. Nowhere in *Of Grammatology*, or anywhere else that I am aware of, does Derrida explicitly concede the fictionality of his account of the history of Western metaphysics, in particular the relationship of speech and writing in that history. And yet if pressed, Derrida would, I suspect, concede that the truth of his account is necessarily provisional—but add that it *is* true nonetheless within an encompassing context of interpretation, that "truth" is made possible by the stability of such contexts, and while

102. Martin Luther, *First Lectures on the Psalms, I: Psalms 1–75*, in *Luther's Works*, vol. 10, ed. Hilton C. Oswald, trans. Herbert J. A. Bouman (St. Louis: Concordia Publishing House, 1974), 399–400; cf. 211ff. Ong does not cite this example; it was a friend, Francis Watson, who drew my attention to it.

103. Walter J. Ong, *The Presence of the Word: Some Prolegomena for Cultural and Religious History* (Minneapolis: University of Minnesota Press, 1981), 138.

104. Ibid., 322.

105. Paul de Man, "The Rhetoric of Blindness: Jacques Derrida's Reading of Rousseau," in *Blindness and Insight: Essays in the Rhetoric of Contemporary Criticism* (2d ed.; Minneapolis: University of Minnesota Press, 1983), 137, his emphasis.

such stability can never be absolute, "it is sometimes so great as to seem immutable and permanent," the "result of a whole history of relations of force."[106] In consequence, a deconstructive reading "must . . . continue (up to a certain point) to respect the rules of that which it deconstructs."[107] Without this apparent contradiction, asks Derrida, "would anything ever be done? Would anything ever be changed?"[108] Or as de Man himself might put it, the deconstructive reading will necessarily be caught (out) "in its own form of blindness," but not without having first produced "its own bright moment of insight."[109]

Derrida has occasionally couched his own bright moment of insight in psychoanalytic terms: "[O]ne can follow the treatment accorded to writing as a particularly revelatory *symptom*, from Plato to Rousseau, Saussure, Husserl, occasionally Heidegger himself."[110] But a symptom of what? "The treatment accorded to writing in the accepted sense serves as a revelatory index of the repression to which archewriting [writing in the generalized sense] is subject."[111] Indeed, "[m]etaphysics has constituted an exemplary system of defense against the threat of writing."[112] At issue is a question of identity, then. The treatment accorded to writing has been "the exclusion by which [the Western tradition] has constituted and recognized itself, from the *Phaedrus* to the *Course in General Linguistics*."[113] To deconstruct that tradition, therefore, would be to think what up to now has been unthinkable, "to think . . . what this history has been able to dissimulate or forbid," "to read all the texts of our culture . . . as kinds of symptoms . . . of something that *could not be presented* in the history of philosophy, and which, moreover, is *nowhere present*, since all of this concerns putting into question the major determination of the meaning of Being

106. Jacques Derrida, "Afterword: Toward an Ethic of Discussion," trans. Samuel Weber, in *Limited Inc* (Evanston, Ill.: Northwestern University Press, 1988), 145; cf. 150–51.

107. Ibid., 152.

108. Ibid.

109. De Man, "The Rhetoric of Blindness," 139.

110. Derrida, *Positions*, 7, emphasis added.

111. Ibid., 8. The speaker in this instance is Henri Ronse, Derrida's interviewer, but Derrida does not quibble with Ronse's formulation of the issue.

112. Derrida, *Of Grammatology*, 101. See further, Jacques Derrida, "Freud and the Scene of Writing," in *Writing and Difference*, esp. 196–98.

113. Ibid., 103.

as *presence*."[114] This "something" that cannot be presented and is nowhere present will turn out, of course, to be arche-writing—another name for *différance*.[115]

THE NON-NAMES OF WHAT SHOULD NOT BE CALLED GOD

Derrida has never ceased to write on *différance*, although *différance* could not remain the same as he did so. In "La Différance" he had predicted that "the efficacy of the thematic of *différance* may very well, indeed must, one day be superseded, lending itself if not to its own replacement, at least to enmeshing itself in a chain that in truth it never will have governed. Whereby, once again, it is not theological."[116] Later in *Positions* we read: "Since it cannot be elevated into a master-word or a master-concept, since it blocks every relationship to theology, *différance* finds itself enmeshed in the work that pulls it through a chain of other 'concepts,' other 'words,' other textual configurations. [T]hey spread out in a chain over the practical and theoretical entirety of a text, and each time in a different way."[117] Each time in a different way, certainly; hence the interest of Derrida's readings. And yet I must admit that as I read and reread these different readings, and reflect on Derrida's definitions of the *différant* terms that he uncovers in the writers he admires, I find that there are only so many different ways to unsay the unsayable.

Of *arche-writing*, for example, a term that arose in part from Derrida's analysis of Freud, one reads that it "is that very thing which cannot let itself be reduced to the form of *presence*."[118] And just as *différance* is "the obliterated origin of absence and presence,"[119] so too arche-writing is said to be a "complicity of origins." "What is lost in that complicity is therefore the myth of the simplicity of origin."[120]

114. Derrida, *Positions*, 6–7, his emphasis.
115. The terms *arche-writing* and *différance* are used synonymously in *Of Grammatology*, 60; cf. *Positions*, 8.
116. Derrida, "Différance," 7.
117. Derrida, *Positions*, 40.
118. Derrida, *Of Grammatology*, 57, his emphasis.
119. Ibid., 143.
120. Ibid., 92.

Then there is the *trace*, a term that emerged from Derrida's readings of Nietzsche, Freud, Heidegger, and the French philosopher Emmanuel Levinas.[121] "Call *trace* that which does not let itself be summed up in the simplicity of a present," he says.[122] And again: "*The (pure) trace is différance.* It does not depend on any sensible plenitude, audible or visible, phonic or graphic. It is, on the contrary, the condition of such a plenitude."[123] "The trace must be thought before the entity," then. But "this formulation is not theological, as one might believe somewhat hastily. The 'theological' is a determined moment in the total movement of the trace."[124] "The trace is in fact the absolute origin of sense in general. Which amounts to saying once again that there is no absolute origin of sense in general."[125]

Pharmakon, supplement, and *hymen* are three further Derridean nonterms, as we have seen, adjacent links on the differantial chain. Derrida stumbled upon them in certain works by Plato, Rousseau, and Mallarmé, respectively. All three terms have "a double, contradictory, undecidable value," for Derrida, which is to say that each inscribes *différance* within itself.[126] The Greek word *pharmakon* can mean "medicine" and "cure" but it can also mean "poison"; *supplement* can mean either an addition that is superfluous or one that is essential; and *hymen* can symbolize the consummation of marriage but also denotes the intact vaginal membrane that indicates that consummation has not yet occurred. What attracts Derrida to these duplicitous terms is that all three are metaphors for writing in the texts in which they occur. "Is it by chance that all these play effects, these 'words' that escape philosophical mastery, should have, in widely differing historical contexts, a very singular relation to writing?" he asks.[127] Derrida's readings of Plato, Rousseau, and Mallarmé are among his finest; they are delicate, intricate, rigorous, and erudite. The renderings of these readings that follow, therefore, are cartoons (although cartoons can be accurate distortions at times).

121. As he explains in *Of Grammatology*, 70.
122. Ibid., 66.
123. Ibid., 62, his emphasis.
124. Ibid., 47.
125. Ibid., 65, emphasis removed.
126. Jacques Derrida, "The Double Session," in *Dissemination*, 221.
127. Ibid.

Early on in Plato's *Phaedrus*, Socrates compares the written text to a *pharmakon*, a drug; thereafter, the term bobs and weaves its way through the dialogue. The burden of Derrida's reading of the *Phaedrus* is to show how the *pharmakon* "is the *différance* of difference,"[128] and as such "the prior medium in which differentiation in general is produced."[129] Writing as a *pharmakon*, therefore, "cannot simply be assigned a site within what it situates, cannot be subsumed under concepts whose contours it draws, leaves only its ghost to a logic that can only seek to govern it insofar as logic arises from it."[130] As such, the *pharmakon* is a "dangerous supplement" to any metaphysical system.[131]

The *supplement* comes into its own, however, only in Derrida's reading of selected texts of Rousseau, in the course of which we learn that "supplementarity . . . is *nothing*, neither a presence nor an absence. . . . It is precisely the play of presence and absence, the opening of this play that no metaphysical or ontological concept can comprehend."[132] Thus we read: "supplement, another name for *différance*."[133] And again: "Writing will appear to us more and more as another name for this structure of supplementarity."[134]

The case is similar with the *hymen*, which features prominently in "The Double Session," Derrida's exuberant reading of a prose poem by Mallarmé. "The hymen never presents itself. It never *is*—in the present."[135] "At the edge of being, the medium of the hymen . . . outwits and outdoes all ontologies."[136]

Other Derridean nonterms include *spacing*, which "designates *nothing*, nothing that is, no presence";[137] *dissemination*, which, as "seminal *différance*," "can be led neither to a present of simple origin . . . nor to an eschatological presence," and "no more presents

---

128. Derrida, "Plato's Pharmacy," 127.
129. Ibid., 126.
130. Ibid., 103.
131. Ibid., 110.
132. Derrida, *Of Grammatology*, 244, his emphasis.
133. Ibid., 150; cf. 315.
134. Ibid., 245.
135. Derrida, "The Double Session," 229, his emphasis.
136. Ibid., 215.
137. Derrida, *Positions*, 81, his emphasis. Recall our earlier discussion of the spatial aspect of *différance*.

than represents itself, no more shows than hides itself";[138] and *parergon*, which crops up in Kant's discussion of art, denotes, among other things, a frame, and elicits such comments from Derrida as: "*There is* frame, but the frame *does not exist*"; "It never lets itself be simply exposed."[139]

The picture I have been sketching is a reductive caricature of the richness of Derridean reading—but it is a caricature that Derrida himself has also indulged in. I have argued that Derrida has written repeatedly, even incessantly, on *différance*, and that this writing has always had an intimate relationship to negative theology. Derrida attempted to forestall rumors of this relationship in his 1968 lecture, "La Différance," as we saw, and he seldom referred to negative theology thereafter. After a lapse of almost twenty years, however, a much-mellowed Derrida presented a follow-up paper at a conference in Jerusalem, a paper devoted exclusively to his curious relationship with negative theology and interspersed with instructive cartoons such as this one:

> Suppose, by a provisional hypothesis, that negative theology consists of considering that every predicative language is inadequate to the essence, in truth to the hyperessentiality (the being beyond Being) of God; consequently, only a negative ("apophatic") attribution can claim to approach God, and to prepare us for a silent intuition of God. By a more or less tenable analogy, one would thus recognize some traits, the family resemblance of negative theology, in every discourse that seems to return in a regular and insistent manner to this rhetoric of negative determination, endlessly multiplying the defenses and the apophatic warnings: this, which is called X (for example, text, writing, the trace, *différance*, the hymen, the supplement, the pharmakon, the parergon, etc.) "is" neither this nor that, neither sensible nor intelligible, neither positive nor negative, neither

138. Ibid., 45, 86–87. Cf. Jacques Derrida, "Dissemination," in *Dissemination*, esp. 268. Dissemination is also identified with writing: "To write—dissemination . . ." (*Positions*, 86).

139. Jacques Derrida, "Parergon," in *The Truth in Painting*, trans. Geoff Bennington and Ian McLeod (Chicago: University of Chicago Press, 1987), 81, 75, his emphasis. The list now runs to some forty or fifty terms. One of the earliest and most important of these is *text*, used in a special sense. For a detailed explanation of this concept, see Rodolphe Gasché, *The Tain of the Mirror: Derrida and the Philosophy of Reflection* (Cambridge, Mass.: Harvard University Press, 1986), 278–93.

inside nor outside, neither superior nor inferior, neither active nor passive, neither present nor absent. . . . Despite appearances, then, this X is neither a concept nor even a name; it does not *lend itself* to a series of names, but calls for another syntax, and exceeds even the order and the structure of predicative discourse. It "is" not and does not say what it "is." It is written completely otherwise.[140]

Does this amount to negative theology or not? In reponse to "accusations" that it does, Derrida gives an oddly indecisive answer, emphatic at first—"No, what I write is not 'negative theology' "—then wavering ever so slightly—"No, I would hesitate to inscribe what I put forward under the familiar heading of negative theology"—then teetering on the brink of outright uncertainty—

I thought I had to forbid myself to write in the register of "negative theology," because I was aware of [its] movement toward hyperessentiality, beyond Being. What *différance*, the *trace*, and so on "mean"—which hence *does not mean anything*—is "before" the concept, the name, the word, "something" that would be nothing, that no longer arises from Being, from presence or from the presence of the present, nor even from absence, and even less from some hyperessentiality. Yet the onto-theological reappropriation always remains possible—and doubtless *inevitable* insofar as one speaks, precisely, in the element of logic and of onto-theological grammar. If the movement of this reappropriation appears in fact irrepressible, its ultimate failure is no less necessary. But I concede that this question remains at the heart of a thinking of *différance*.[141]

I take all of this to mean that Derrida has always aspired to a writing that would be "beyond" negative theology, while recognizing that this might not be possible. After all, by his own admission, "*différance* remains a metaphysical name" when all is unsaid and undone.[142] Although separated from negative theology, therefore, his writing is by no means divorced from it. And his passion for negative theology has clearly increased over the years. If it was the subject of an apology in "La Différance," it is the subject of a eulogy in his most

140. Jacques Derrida, "How to Avoid Speaking: Denials," trans. Ken Frieden, in *Derrida and Negative Theology*, 74, his emphasis.

141. Ibid., 77, 78, 79, his emphasis.

142. Derrida, "Différance," 26. Cf. his "Ellipsis," in *Writing and Difference*, where he also seems to concede the impossibility of exceeding negative theology or its "accomplice," "negative atheology" (297).

recent discussion of it, a "Post-Scriptum" to the collection *Derrida and Negative Theology*. The postscript ends with an unmistakable *au revoir*: "Negative theology, we have said this enough, is also the most economical and most powerful formalization, the greatest reserve of language possible in so few words. Inexhaustible literature, literature for the desert, for the exile, always saying too much and too little, it holds desire in suspense. It always leaves you without ever going away from you."[143] Imperceptibly over the years, it seems, cold suspicion has warmed into outright infatuation.

This infatuation has yet to yield an ethics, however, and as such it leaves itself open to the accusation that it is a pursuit without practical consequences. Certainly, *direct* engagement with the ethico-political domain has always been the exception rather than the rule for Derrida. But that does not mean that deconstruction is incapable of being diverted into this domain, as we have seen. What might deconstruction mean for a feminist reading of the Gospels, for example? It is time we tested the water, specifically the living water that is the subject of the longest dialogue between Jesus and a woman in the canonical Gospels.

143. Jacques Derrida, "Post-Scriptum: Aporias, Ways and Voices," trans. John P. Leavey, Jr., in *Derrida and Negative Theology*, 321–22.

2

DECONSTRUCTIVE CRITICISM: DERRIDA ᴬᵀ_ᴛʜᴇ SAMARITAN WELL AND, LATER, ᴬᵀ_ᴛʜᴇ FOOT OF THE CROSS

JESUS, weary from his journey, is sitting on the lip of the well. The Samaritan woman arrives to draw water. The crowd parts to let her through. Some have brought binoculars, others are already taking notes.

JESUS' DESIRE

For many who have written on the scene at the Samaritan well in John 4, the woman's oblivion to her own need, so much greater than that of Jesus, is the pivot on which the irony turns. Paul D. Duke, for example, remarks, "Jesus greets the woman with a request for water (cf. Gen. 24:17), an irony in itself in view of who will eventually give water to whom."[1]

Gail R. O'Day elaborates: "She assumes that she is in conversation with a thirsty Jew; this Jew informs her that if she knew both the gift of God and the identity of the person with whom she was speaking, she would recognize that she herself was the thirsty one."[2]

1. Paul D. Duke, *Irony in the Fourth Gospel* (Atlanta: John Knox Press, 1985), 101.
2. Gail R. O'Day, *Revelation in the Fourth Gospel: Narrative Mode and Theological Claim* (Philadelphia: Fortress Press, 1986), 60.

Teresa Okure concurs:

> In Jesus' case, his exercise of humility is outstanding by the fact that though he is the one with "the gift of God" to offer (v 10), he nonetheless approaches the woman as a beggar. . . . Ironically . . . the woman is the one who needs to drink. Jesus' thirst and her as yet unrecognized thirst are thus inseparably linked. . . . The whole point of v 10, therefore, is that if only the woman knew it, she, not Jesus, is the beggar who needs to ask and receive from him the gift of eternal life, given freely for the asking.[3]

Raymond E. Brown distills the dialogue thus: "*Jesus* asks the Samaritan for water, violating the social customs of the time. . . . *Woman* mocks Jesus for being so in need that he does not observe the proprieties. . . . *Jesus* shows that the real reason for his action is not his inferiority or need, but his superior status."[4]

Rudolf Schnackenburg is yet more blunt: "It is not Jesus who is in need of anything, but the woman; and she is confronted with the one person who can satisfy the deepest needs of man."[5] But are Jesus' own needs in this scene really any less than those of the woman?

"Give me a drink," says Jesus. The demand would appear to be double. Seated wearily at a well whose water is beyond his reach, Jesus desires a drink. But he has another desire that well water cannot satisfy, as 4:10 suggests: "If you knew the gift of God, and who it is that is saying to you, 'Give me a drink,' you would have asked him, and he would have given you living water." What Jesus longs for from this woman, even more than delicious spring water, is that *she* long for the living water that *he* longs to give *her*.[6] Jesus thirsts to arouse *her* thirst. His desire is to arouse her desire, to be himself desired. His desire is to be the desire of this woman, to have her recognize in him that which she herself lacks. His desire is to fill up *her* lack. Only thus can his own deeper thirst be assuaged, his own lack be filled. To this

3. Teresa Okure, *The Johannine Approach to Mission: A Contextual Study of John 4:1-42* (Tübingen: J. C. B. Mohr [Paul Siebeck], 1988), 86–87, 95, 98.

4. Raymond E. Brown, *The Gospel According to John (I–XII)* (Garden City, N.Y.: Doubleday, 1966), 177, his emphasis.

5. Rudolf Schnackenburg, *The Gospel According to St. John*, trans. Kevin Smyth et al. (New York: Herder and Herder, 1968), 1:426.

6. Cf. Okure, *The Johannine Approach to Mission*, 95.

lack, one of several holes around which my reading is organized, I shall later return.[7]

SIZING UP THE OPPOSITIONS

The Samaritan woman appears to be incapable of distinguishing the literal and material from the figurative and spiritual. "Sir," she finally says, "give me this water, so that I may never be thirsty or have to keep coming here to draw water" (4:15). A two-story ironic structure is thereby erected.[8] Below, at ground level, is the apparent meaning, in which the woman, as unwitting victim, is trapped. It would seem that the only door in this ironic structure leads upstairs, although the woman has yet to discover it. Above is a higher level of meaning, a second floor of which the woman is unaware, unlike the reading or listening audience, who have just now taken up residence there along with Jesus and the Johannine narrator, who share a double bed.

This two-story structure is a hierarchical opposition. The Fourth Gospel contains row upon row of such structures. The road to the well, for example, is lined with them: knowledge/ignorance (1:10, 26, 31; 3:10-11; cf. 1:18), spiritual/literal (2:19-21; 3:3-4), spirit/flesh (3:6; cf. 1:13), heavenly things (*ta epourania*)/earthly things (*ta epigeia*) (3:12; cf. 3:31), light/darkness (3:19-21; cf. 1:7-9), baptism in the Holy Spirit/water baptism (1:31-33; cf. 3:5), miraculous wine/water for ritual cleansing (2:6ff.), heavenly ascent/descent (1:51; 3:13; cf. 3:31), and so on.

As much as anything, deconstruction is a dismantling of "the binary oppositions of metaphysics," as we have seen.[9] Of course, all oppositions are not created equal. "Each pair operates with very different stakes in the world," as Barbara Johnson has observed.[10] The

---

7. This language of lack and desire is adapted from Jacques Lacan. See Further Reading for a bibliography on Lacan.

8. To use a metaphor beloved of the literary commentators; see esp. R. Alan Culpepper, *Anatomy of the Fourth Gospel: A Study in Literary Design* (Philadelphia: Fortress Press, 1983), 167–68, and Duke, *Irony in the Fourth Gospel*, 13–14. The metaphor seems to have originated with D. C. Muecke; see *The Compass of Irony* (London: Methuen, 1969), 19.

9. Derrida, *Positions*, 41.

10. Barbara Johnson, *A World of Difference* (Baltimore: Johns Hopkins University Press, 1987), 2.

exchange between Jesus and the woman of Samaria, an ironic two-tiered structure according to the majority reading, is itself housed within a much larger enclosure, that of the opposition between male and female, a gigantic pavilion whose stakes extend very deep into the world indeed.

DECONSTRUCTION AND FEMINISM

The Samaritan woman contrasts sharply with Jesus' previous conversation partner. "When Jesus speaks with Nicodemus in John 3, he speaks with a male member of the Jewish religious establishment. In John 4 he speaks with a female member of an enemy people," notes O'Day. "Nicodemus has a name, but the woman is unnamed; she is known only by what she is—a foreign woman."[11] The conversation between Jesus and the woman is, of course, a scandalous one, as O'Day goes on to remark; Jewish men were not supposed to speak with Samaritan women (4:9, 27),[12] and Jewish rabbis (4:31) were not supposed to speak in public with any kind of woman.[13] Jesus breaches this double boundary by engaging the Samaritan woman in conversation.

In addition to O'Day, at least two other feminist scholars, Regina St. G. Plunkett and Sandra M. Schneiders, have recently advanced readings of this scene.[14] Despite substantial differences of approach, the common burden of all three readings has been to redress the ill-treatment that the Samaritan woman has endured at the hands of male interpreters. The issue centers on Jesus' "prophetic" declaration

11. Gail R. O'Day, "John," in *The Women's Bible Commentary*, ed. Carol A. Newsom and Sharon H. Ringe (Louisville: Westminster/John Knox Press, 1992), 295.

12. "The daughters of the Samaritans are menstruants from their cradle [i.e., perpetually unclean]" (*Niddah* 4.1). Cited in C. K. Barrett, *The Gospel According to St. John* (2d ed.; Philadelphia: Westminster Press, 1978), 232.

13. For the rabbinic sources, see Barrett, *The Gospel According to St. John*, 240.

14. Regina St. G. Plunkett, "The Samaritan Woman: Partner in Revelation," unpublished paper presented at the New England regional meeting of the Society of Biblical Literature, Boston, March 1988; and Sandra M. Schneiders, *The Revelatory Text: Interpreting the New Testament as Sacred Scripture* (San Francisco: HarperCollins, 1991), 180–99.

to the woman, "You have had five husbands, and the one you have now is not your husband" (4:18; cf. 4:19). Should this statement be taken literally, that is, as a statement about an irregular marital and sexual career?[15] The literal reading has resulted in some curious comments, ranging, in modern times, from Theodor Zahn's reference to the woman's "immoral life, which has exhibited profligacy and unbridled passions for a long time," to Paul Duke's description of her as "a five-time loser . . . currently committed to an illicit affair."[16] Or should the verse be read figuratively instead, that is, as a statement about the religious infidelity of Samaria itself, represented here by the woman? Samaria had worshiped the gods of five foreign tribes (cf. 2 Kings 17:13-34) and apparently its current Yahwism was also adulterated ("the one you have now is not your husband"). This has been the dominant form of the figurative or symbolic reading.[17]

15. The literal reading need not lead inevitably to this conclusion, however. O'Day recasts the literal reading as follows: "The text does not say . . . that the woman has been divorced five times but that she has had five husbands. There are many possible reasons for the woman's marital history. . . . Perhaps the woman, like Tamar in Genesis 38, is trapped in the custom of levirate marriage and the last male in the family line has refused to marry her" ("John," 296).

16. Theodor Zahn, *Das Evangelium des Johannes ausgelegt* (6th ed.; Leipzig: Deichert, 1921), 244; Duke, *Irony in the Fourth Gospel*, 102. Others assume more generally that Jesus is "lay[ing] bare the woman's sin" (E. C. Hoskyns, *The Fourth Gospel*, ed. F. N. Davey [2d ed.; London: Faber and Faber, 1947], 242), that he has "exposed her bawdy past" (Jeffrey Lloyd Staley, *The Print's First Kiss: A Rhetorical Investigation of the Implied Reader in the Fourth Gospel* [Atlanta: Scholars Press, 1988], 101) or her "immoral life" (George R. Beasley-Murray, *John* [Waco: Word Books, 1987], 61), that she is "wayward" (Schnackenburg, *The Gospel According to St. John*, 1:433), "of low morals" (Birger Olsson, *Structure and Meaning in the Fourth Gospel: A Text-Linguistic Analysis of John 2:1-11 and 4:1-42* [Lund: CWK Gleerup, 1974], 120), "markedly immoral" and a doer of "evil deeds" (Brown, *The Gospel According to John (I–XII)*, 171, 177), "loose living" (C. H. Dodd, *The Interpretation of the Fourth Gospel* [Cambridge: Cambridge University Press, 1968], 313), and so on. Lyle Eslinger goes further, arguing that the woman, whom he calls "coquettish," "coy," "lascivious," "brazen," and "carnal," makes "sexual advances" to Jesus ("The Wooing of the Woman at the Well: Jesus, the Reader and Reader-Response Criticism," *Literature and Theology* 1 [1987]: 171, 177–78).

17. And it is the one that Schneiders strongly favors (*The Revelatory Text*, 190–91, 195).

What might deconstruction contribute to this debate? At least two insights. First, deconstruction tends to work with the heuristic assumption that the literary text is capable of deftly turning the tables on the critic who sets out to master it. The critic, while appearing to grasp the meaning of the text from a position safely outside or above it, has unknowingly been grasped by the text and pulled into it. He or she is unwittingly acting out an interpretive role that the text has scripted in advance. As Shoshana Felman puts it, introducing a highly effective demonstration of such conscription: "The scene of the critical debate is thus a *repetition* of the scene dramatized in the text. The critical interpretation, in other words, not only elucidates the text but also reproduces it dramatically, unwittingly *participates in it*. Through its very reading, the text, so to speak, acts itself out."[18]

How does this apply to our scene? The majority of Johannine commentators have preferred the literal reading of 4:18 to the figurative one. These have included such authorities as C. K. Barrett, G. R. Beasley-Murray, Raymond Brown, Rudolf Bultmann, Ernst Haenchen, Barnabas Lindars, and Rudolf Schnackenburg.[19] At the same time, these commentators have scrupulously noted the repeated failure of the woman to grasp the nonliteral nature of Jesus' discourse. In opting to take Jesus' statement in 4:18 at face value, then, they effectively trade places with the woman. They reenact what they purport to be describing. They mimic the literal-mindedness that marks her as inferior in their eyes. The standard reading of 4:18 conceals a double standard, then. To interpret Jesus literally is a failing when the woman

18. Shoshana Felman, "Turning the Screw of Interpretation," in *Literature and Psychoanalysis. The Question of Reading: Otherwise*, ed. Shoshana Felman (Baltimore: Johns Hopkins University Press, 1982), 101, her emphasis. Her text is Henry James's *The Turn of the Screw*. For similar quotations from Derrida, Paul de Man, J. Hillis Miller, and Barbara Johnson, and for a discussion of Mark and its interpreters from this perspective, see my *Mark and Luke*, 28–38.

19. See Barrett, *The Gospel According to St. John*, 235; Beasley-Murray, *John*, 61; Brown, *The Gospel of John (I–XII)*, 171; Rudolf Bultmann, *The Gospel of John*, trans. G. R. Beasley-Murray, R. W. N. Hoare, and J. K. Riches (Philadelphia: Westminster Press, 1971), 187; Ernst Haenchen, *John 1: A Commentary on the Gospel of John Chapters 1–6*, trans. Robert W. Funk with Ulrich Busse (Philadelphia: Fortress Press, 1984), 221; Barnabas Lindars, *The Gospel of John* (London: Marshall, Morgan & Scott, 1972), 185; and Schnackenburg, *The Gospel According to St. John*, 1:433.

does it, but not when the commentators follow suit. This double standard is, however, also a double bind. They can condemn her only if they participate in her error, can ascribe a history of immorality to her only by reading as "carnally" as she does—at which point the literal reading of 4:18 threatens to become a displaced reenactment of yet another Johannine episode, one in which an unnamed woman is similarly charged with sexual immorality by accusers who themselves stand accused (8:1-11).

Let us move on to a second, more substantial contribution that deconstruction can make to the nascent feminist debate on John 4. Traditionally, commentators have tended to view the Samaritan woman's literal-minded responses to Jesus' pronouncements as a rich example of Johannine irony. Tellingly, Schneiders makes no mention of irony in her reading of John 4:4-42, nor does O'Day in her reading of it in *The Women's Bible Commentary*, although O'Day's earlier study of the episode in her book, *Revelation in the Fourth Gospel*, was precisely a study of its irony.[20] And Regina Plunkett has argued that, contrary to appearances, the Samaritan woman is not in fact a victim of irony.[21] The word "victim" is significant here. Recent feminist readers of John 4:1-42 have been countering a traditional tendency on the part of male commentators to victimize the Samaritan woman—to reduce her to a sexual stereotype, to patronize her for her intellectual "inferiority"[22]—thereby providing yet another biblical warrant for the unequal treatment of contemporary women in the church, the academy, and society at large.[23] The challenge would seem to be that of showing that the Samaritan woman is indeed a worthy conversation partner for Jesus, and this O'Day, Plunkett, and Schneiders undertake to do, each in her own way.[24] "The woman is the first character in the Gospel to engage in serious theological conversation with Jesus," concludes

20. See O'Day, *Revelation in the Fourth Gospel*, 49–92.

21. Plunkett, "The Samaritan Woman."

22. Examples of the latter also abound; two will suffice to give the general idea. Dodd remarks on 4:15 that the woman, "as usual, fails to understand," indicating "a crass inability to penetrate below the surface meaning" (*The Interpretation of the Fourth Gospel*, 313). For Beasley-Murray, too, at this point, "the woman's misunderstanding becomes crass" (*John*, 61).

23. Cf. Schneiders, *The Revelatory Text*, 188, and O'Day, "John," 296.

24. This is also the task that Teresa Okure takes on, as we shall see.

O'Day.[25] Schneiders goes further: "Nowhere in the fourth gospel is there a dialogue of such theological depth and intensity," she claims.[26]

What remains unquestioned in these readings, however, is Jesus' superiority to the Samaritan woman. He retains his privileged role as the dispenser of knowledge—"the subject presumed to know," as Jacques Lacan would say—while the woman retains her traditional role as the compliant recipient of knowledge, a container as empty as her water jar, waiting to be filled. The hierarchical opposition of male and female—the male in the missionary position, the female beneath—remains essentially undisturbed. And as long as this hierarchy remains intact, Jesus' boundary-breaching activity and challenge to the status quo in this episode, while not inconsequential, remains a minor tremor rather than a major upheaval. But what if the Samaritan woman were found to be the more enlightened partner in the dialogue from the outset? What if her insight were found to exceed that of Jesus all along? Impossible? Not at all, as I hope to show.

Before proceeding with my reading, however, I would like to situate it more precisely in relation to other forms of feminist exegesis. Susan Durber has recently provided a rough but useful sketch of the scene.[27] "There is a kind of feminist approach to the biblical texts," she notes, "which admits that there are many points at which they are indefensibly sexist, but argues that, at their crowning moments, they declare or hint at a message of liberation for women and point to a fundamental overturning of the oppression of women." For example, "Isaiah uses some female imagery, Paul declared that in Christ there was no difference between male and female, and, most notably, Jesus displayed an uncommonly kind attitude to women, even including them among his disciples (though not the Twelve) and entrusting them first with the good news of his resurrection."[28] O'Day and Schneiders could

25. O'Day, "John," 296.
26. Schneiders, *The Revelatory Text*, 191.
27. Susan Durber, "The Female Reader of the Parables of the Lost," *Journal for the Study of the New Testament* 45 (1992): 59ff. For a more detailed survey, see Janice Capel Anderson, "Mapping Feminist Biblical Criticism: The American Scene, 1983–1990," *Critical Review of Books in Religion* 4 (1991): 21–44. The scene is actually quite complex, because many women of color doing work in this mode reject the label "feminist," believing it to have white, elitist connotations, and prefer such self-designations as *womanist* (if they are African-American) or *mujerista* (if they are Hispanic).
28. Durber, "The Female Reader of the Parables of the Lost," 59.

be said to exemplify this kind of feminist approach; O'Day's discussion, for example, leads to the conclusion that the Samaritan woman is "a witness and disciple like John the Baptist, Andrew, and Philip."[29] Okure, too, while she does not label her reading a feminist one, writes of Jesus' "humble approach which gives the advantage to the dialogue partner," and of his "deep respect for the woman."[30]

Durber is much more critical of the Jesus refracted in the Gospels, joining Daphne Hampson in arguing that "although Jesus was not a misogynist, neither was he in any sense a feminist, even according to a most minimal definition. There is no evidence at all that he mounted a critique of the position of women in his society." Ultimately he failed to "challenge male privilege."[31] Durber "reluctantly" questions "the idea that the biblical texts can be reclaimed and reinterpreted for feminists or, indeed, for women." She intends "to show that the biblical texts are by and for men" and "how they continue, every time they are read, to sustain the practice of the dominance of men over women known as patriarchy."[32] To do this, she will draw "from a variety of poststructuralist thought."[33] Her ensuing reading of the "parables of the lost" in Luke 15 is, to my knowledge, the most thoroughgoing adaptation to date of French poststructuralism for feminist biblical exegesis.[34]

29. O'Day, "John," 296. Schneiders's conclusions are similar (*The Revelatory Text*, 192–94). Cf. Elisabeth Schüssler-Fiorenza, *In Memory of Her: A Feminist Theological Reconstruction of Christian Origins* (New York: Crossroad, 1983), 138.

30. Okure, *The Johannine Approach to Mission*, 186.

31. Durber, "The Female Reader of the Parables of the Lost," 59–60. Cf. Daphne Hampson, *Theology and Feminism* (Oxford: Basil Blackwell, 1979).

32. Durber, "The Female Reader of the Parables of the Lost," 60.

33. Ibid.

34. She enlists Julia Kristeva, Jacques Lacan, Louis Althusser, and Jacques Derrida. Other examples of feminist poststructuralist exegesis include Kerry M. Craig and Margret A. Kristjansson, "Women Reading as Men/Women Reading as Women," *Semeia* 51 (1990): 119–36; Susan Lochrie Graham, "Silent Voices: Women in the Gospel of Mark," *Semeia* 54 (1991): 145–58; and Elizabeth A. Castelli, "Interpretations of Power in 1 Corinthians," *Semeia* 54 (1991): 197–222. Feminism and poststructuralism frequently combine in the writings of Mieke Bal also; see esp. *Death and Dissymmetry: The Politics of Coherence in the Book of Judges* (Chicago: University of Chicago Press, 1988).

I admire what Durber has done, and yet I would argue that a poststructuralist reading of a biblical text can lead in other directions as well, that it need not always amount to a demonstration of how the text reinscribes the dominance of men over women. While I tend to agree with Durber that "the biblical texts are by and for men,"[35] I would argue, and hope to show, that deconstruction, in particular, can enable us to read against the grain of the biblical authors' intentions in ways that affirm women.[36]

THE HYDRAULICS OF A LIQUID METAPHOR

We will not, as do positive historians, account for all that could have flowed into this text *from the outside.*

—*Jacques Derrida*[37]

The issue in John 4:7-15 can be refocused as follows. Two kinds of water, literal and figurative, slosh around in the Samaritan woman's head, it would seem, mingling where they should not (vv. 11-12, 15). For me, however, the real question is whether Jesus himself can keep the living water pure and clear, uncontaminated by the profane drinking water. To discover the answer we shall have to track the course of this water downstream. It flows underground through the Gospel, for the most part, surfacing again only in chapters 7 and 19. To these water-stained pages we now turn.

On the last day of the feast of Tabernacles, "the great day," Jesus again speaks of thirst, drinking, and the supramundane living water: "As the scripture has said, 'Out of his heart [lit. belly] shall flow rivers of living water [*potamoi ek tēs koilias autou rheusousin hudatos zōntos*]'" (7:38, RSV). Out of whose heart? Jesus' heart or that of the believer? The earlier exchange at the well would seem to authorize either reading. In 4:10 Jesus pointed to himself as the source of the living water. Rivers of living water might therefore be said to flow out of him. But he added that once the believer has drunk of this water, it becomes a spring in him or her "gushing up to eternal life"

---

35. Durber, "The Female Reader of the Parables of the Lost," 60.
36. I am not alone in this opinion, needless to say. Graham, for example, has also drawn on deconstruction in order to pit the Marcan text against its author ("Silent Voices," esp. 147).
37. Derrida, "Qual Quelle," 275, his emphasis.

(4:14). Rivers of living water can also be said to flow out of the believer, then—but only if the believer has first been filled with the water that issues forth from Jesus. The believer is more than a mere receptacle for surplus water, therefore, an overflow; rather, he or she is a channel, or conduit, in his or her own right.[38]

Let us return to the feast of Tabernacles. We may still be in time to see the procession enter through the Water Gate and the priest pour out the daily water libation.[39] Surrounded by so much water we cannot refrain from asking, Is Jesus really the origin of the living water in the Fourth Gospel? Is he the spring, the source, from which it flows? As we have seen, Jesus attempts to authorize himself as the source by appealing to scripture ("As the scripture has said [*kathōs eipen hē graphē*] . . . "). In so doing, however, he inadvertently creates a rival. Might this scriptural verse not itself be the real source of the living water imagery in the Fourth Gospel, the water that first springs up in the course of Jesus' discourse at the Samaritan well (4:10)? In that case, Jesus would himself be a mere conduit for a stream that originated elsewhere, that flowed into this Gospel from outside it. But if this verse *is* the source of the living water in the Fourth Gospel, it is a hidden source. The words "quoted" by Jesus have no exact parallel either in the Masoretic text or the Septuagint. Equipped with divining rods, Johannine scholars have combed all the relevant fields, ranging from the Jewish Scriptures and the rabbinic commentaries to the parched desert region of the Dead Sea Scrolls, but their findings have been inconclusive at best.[40]

This particular source-hunt can be considered paradigmatic of the many source-hunts of historical criticism. The elusive source-text in this instance is itself about a source, a water source ("Out of

38. Deconstruction is "very interested in reading the logic of metaphors, absolutely literally" (Gayatri Chakravorty Spivak, "The New Historicism, Political Commitment and the Postmodern Critic," in *The Post-Colonial Critic: Interviews, Strategies, Dialogues*, ed. Sarah Harasym [New York: Routledge, 1990], 164). In the present context this interest will take the form of swimming with the current of the Johannine water imagery and seeing where it takes us. And it will involve writing a critical text that is itself saturated with water images.

39. See Barrett, *The Gospel According to St. John*, 327, for details of the rite.

40. For a recent report, see Beasley-Murray, *John*, 116–17.

his belly shall flow rivers of living water"), and a highly elusive source at that, if the owner of the belly is Jesus.[41] In the preceding scene, the text has Jesus say to those who would "seize" (*piazō*) him, "You will search for me, but you will not find me" (7:34, 36; cf. 8:21; 13:33). Once again, the text has thematized and dramatized its own reception, the commentators *on* the text inadvertently taking up positions *within* the text.

To the reintroduction of the figure of living water in 7:38 the Johannine narrator adds an important gloss; he interprets the figure as being "about the Spirit, which believers in him were to receive" (7:39). The narrative depiction of that reception is deferred, however: "as yet there was no Spirit [*oupō gar ēn pneuma*], because Jesus was not yet glorified" (7:39).[42] Jesus' glorification will be interpreted in turn as the hour of his exaltation on the cross, an exaltation that will prefigure his resurrection (12:23-24, 28; 13:31-32; 17:1, 5; cf. 3:14; 12:32).

CAPSIZING THE OPPOSITIONS

The motifs of thirst and drinking well up once again as Jesus hangs dying on the cross. More precisely, it is desire that wells up, ostensibly desire for a drink. "I am thirsty," cries the source of the living water (19:28), and we are back once more at the well ("Give me a drink"; 4:7).[43] Again it is about noon (4:6; 19:14),[44] and again Jesus needs more than just a drink. Recall that in the earlier scene Jesus' real desire was to complete the desire of the woman, to fill up that which she lacked. In the crucifixion scene, we can assume that Jesus is physically thirsty, as in 4:7, but the context also suggests a more consuming thirst.

41. The belly may also belong to the believer, as we saw, in which case Jesus and the believer are Siamese twins.
42. See Werner H. Kelber, "In the Beginning Were the Words: The Apotheosis and Narrative Displacement of the Logos," *Journal of the American Academy of Religion* 58 (1990): 88. It was Kelber who initially impelled me to track the course of the living water through John 4, 7, and 19.
43. R. H. Lightfoot notes this connection; 4:7 and 19:28 beg comparison, "these being the only two passages in John which allude to thirst on [Jesus'] part" (*St. John's Gospel*, ed. C. F. Evans [Oxford: Oxford University Press, 1956], 122).
44. Ibid.

According to the narrator, Jesus announces his thirst "in order to fulfill the scripture [*hina teleiōthē hē graphē*]." Here, as at Cana (2:6-10), well water has been replaced with wine (19:29). It has sometimes been asked whether this sour wine or vinegar (*oxos*) offered to Jesus would not have aggravated his thirst rather than quenched it.[45] But his deeper thirst is assuaged, nonetheless. What is essential is that the drink be drawn from Scripture ("He said in order to fulfill the scripture, 'I am thirsty' "), and assuredly this one is (cf. Psalm 69[68]:22, LXX: "for my thirst they gave me *oxos*"). Having accepted the drink, Jesus announces, "It is finished," and expires (19:30). He has fulfilled the Scripture, completed it, made up what was lacking in it.[46] The following homology emerges: as the wine is to the well water, so is Scripture to the Samaritan woman, Jesus' desire drifting between all four terms. But in bringing his desire to completion, has Jesus allowed common *oxos*, "the inferior popular drink,"[47] to mingle with the living water, thereby compromising its purity? It is time we tested a sample of this living water.

Announcing "It is finished," Jesus yields up—what? His spirit? The Spirit? (The Greek simply has *to pneuma*, which could mean either.) The Spirit is not formally handed over until 20:22: "he breathed on them and said to them, 'Receive the Holy Spirit.' " We need not drop "Spirit" from our reading of 19:30 on that account, however; both meanings can be kept in the air at once. This in fact is what Raymond Brown does, taking *to pneuma* in 19:30 to be yet another Johannine double entendre:

> In vii 39 John affirmed that those who believed in Jesus were to receive the Spirit once Jesus had been glorified, and so it would not

45. Barrett responds: "If this was so one wonders why the soldiers drank it" (*The Gospel According to St. John*, 553).

46. In place of the more usual *plēroō* (e.g., 19:24, 36), John uses *teleioō* here for "to fulfill (Scripture)." Since John also uses *teleioō* for the completion of Jesus' work (e.g., 17:4, 23; cf. 19:30), several commentators have suggested that its use in 19:28 means that Scripture is brought to complete fulfillment as Jesus dies (e.g., Brown, *The Gospel According to John (XIII–XXI)*, 908–9). Interestingly, *teleioō* is also used of the completion of Jesus' work in the discourse at the well (4:34). Lightfoot connects 4:34 with 19:30 (*St. John's Gospel*, 122), as does Schnackenburg (*The Gospel According to St. John*, 3:283).

47. Schnackenburg, *The Gospel According to St. John*, 3:283.

be inappropriate that at this climactic moment in the hour of glorification there would be a symbolic reference to the giving of the Spirit. . . . This symbolic reference is evocative and *proleptic*, reminding the reader of the *ultimate* purpose for which Jesus has been lifted up on the cross.[48]

We are now in a position to capsize the hierarchical opposition that established the parameters of the dialogue between Jesus and the Samaritan woman, that between literal and living water, an opposition closely linked to several others, as we saw, such as spiritual/material, heavenly/earthly, and even male/female, given the context. As Jesus dies on the cross, these hierarchies are teetering, about to topple over, needing only the slightest push from us. Having requested a last drink, as prescribed by Scripture, Jesus declares "It is completed," after which he dies and gives up the *pneuma* (his spirit/the Spirit). The satiation of Jesus' physical thirst, therefore, is the necessary precondition for the proleptic yielding up of that which is intended to satiate the *spiritual* thirst of the believer, namely, the Holy Spirit (see 7:37-39; cf. 4:10, 13-14). But it is an arrestingly strange precondition.[49]

In the dialogue at the Samaritan well, the earthly, material, literal level, represented by the thirst for spring water, was declared superseded by a heavenly, spiritual reality, represented by the living water, and thrust into the background. But this material, literal domain is curiously reinstated at the hour of Jesus' glorification, again in the form of physical thirst, now decreed by Scripture, and coupled with physical death. The repressed has made a forceful return. The material order has reasserted itself as the necessary precondition that enables the Spirit, emblem and emissary of the spiritual order (cf. 14:16-17, 26; 15:26; 16:13-15), to come into being for believers (cf. 7:39: "for as yet there was no Spirit [*oupō gar ēn pneuma*], because Jesus was not yet glorified").[50] The hierarchical opposition established at the well is inverted at the cross, the ostensibly superior, pleromatic term (living

48. Brown, *The Gospel According to John (XIII–XXI)*, 931, his emphasis.

49. Cf. Kelber, "In the Beginning Were the Words," 88.

50. As has often been remarked, no distinction is made between ontology and soteriology in 7:39b, the Spirit being presented as though it had no effective existence prior to Jesus' glorification (notwithstanding 1:32!). See further S. H. Hooke, "The Spirit Was Not Yet," *New Testament Studies* 9 (1962–63): 372–80.

water, Spirit) being shown to depend for its effective existence on the inferior, insufficient term (literal well water), contrary to everything that the Gospel has led us to expect: "What is born of the flesh is flesh, and what is born of the Spirit is spirit" (3:6).[51]

DROWNING THE OPPOSITIONS

To content oneself simply with overturning a hierarchical opposition, however, "is still to operate on the terrain of and from within the deconstructed system," according to Derrida.[52] It is still to think in oppositional, hierarchical categories, even if what was once faceup is now facedown, even if the opposition is now floating on its belly instead of its back. It is to continue to reside "within the closed field of these oppositions," thereby confirming its power.[53] A second phase is necessary, one that would entail "the irruptive emergence of a new 'concept,' a concept that can no longer be, and never could be, included in the previous regime," that would inhabit the opposition only to resist and paralyze it.[54]

Sure enough, as if on cue, such a concept makes its appearance immediately after the scene we have been discussing. The proleptic yielding up of the Spirit ("he gave up the *pneuma*"), which is to say the living water (cf. 7:39), is followed by the reemergence of material water, long gone underground, as Jesus' side is pierced and blood and water issue forth (19:34). "Here the paradoxical thing is not the blood but the water,"[55] and the latter has provoked a stream of supraliteral interpretations down through the ages.[56] The modern rationalizations of pathologists and surgeons have done nothing to staunch the flow.[57]

51. Cf. 1:13; 3:31; 4:13-14, 24, 33-34; 6:26-27, 31-33, 49-50, 58, 63; 8:23; 12:25; 17:2.

52. Derrida, *Positions*, 42.

53. Ibid.

54. Ibid., 42–43. Derrida's term for these concepts is *undecidables*, several of which we discussed in chap. 1 (*pharmakon, supplement, hymen,* etc.).

55. Bultmann, *The Gospel of John*, 678 n. 1.

56. See Brown, *The Gospel According to John (XIII–XXI)*, 946–52, and Schnackenburg, *The Gospel According to St. John*, 3:289–90, for examples.

57. For a recent example, see W. D. Edwards, W. J. Gabel, and F. E. Hosmer, "On the Physical Death of Jesus Christ," *Journal of the American Medical Association* 255 (1986): 1455–63.

Some connection between the water discourse of 7:37-39 and the issue of water in 19:34 has often been suggested.[58] Intermingled with the former passage, as we have seen, are the water libations that formed part of the ritual of Tabernacles. Given the association of earthly water with living water and the Spirit, therefore, not only in the Tabernacles discourse and the dialogue at the Samaritan well but also in the dialogue with Nicodemus (3:5), the flow of water from Jesus' side can be read as, among other things, a further token of the promised living water or Spirit, which has now become available through Jesus' glorification. That leaves us with a symbol (the flow of water) of a metaphor (living water) for the Spirit.[59]

When water reappears in this Gospel from an unexpected quarter, therefore—Jesus' side—following an extended drought, it is as an "undecidable" term that fills the literal and figurative categories or containers simultaneously, along with the material and spiritual containers and the earthly and heavenly containers, in such a way as to flood these hierarchical structures and put them temporarily out of commission. Let me attempt to clarify this statement by retracing the stream yet again. At the Samaritan well, literal earthly water was declared superseded by figurative living water (4:13-14), which was later interpreted as the Holy Spirit (7:39), which has now become available through Jesus' death as symbolized both by his giving up the *pneuma* as he expires (19:30) and by the fresh flow of water from his side (19:34). But this water is neither simply material and literal, since it is symbolic, nor fully spiritual and figurative, since it is physical. It is a spiritual material and a literal figure. Literality and figurality intermingle in the flow from Jesus' side, each contaminating the other,

---

58. See, e.g., Barrett, *The Gospel According to St. John*, 556; Bultmann, *The Gospel of John*, 678 n. 1; Dodd, *The Interpretation of the Fourth Gospel*, 428; Hoskyns, *The Fourth Gospel*, 532; and esp. Brown, *The Gospel According to John (XIII–XXI)*, 949–50.

59. Taking "symbol" in its simplest sense as "a visible token of something other than itself" (C. K. Barrett, "Symbolism," in *Essays on John* [Philadelphia: Westminster Press, 1982], 66). Equally simply, I am taking "metaphor" to mean "a transfer of meaning from the word that properly possesses it to another word which belongs to some shared category of meaning" (Thomas McLaughlin, "Figurative Language," in *Critical Terms for Literary Study*, ed. Frank Lentricchia and Thomas McLaughlin [Chicago: University of Chicago Press, 1990], 83).

which is to say that we cannot keep the literal clearly separate from the figurative in the end.

Significantly, the water that dissolves this distinction is part of Jesus' own body, as much a part of it as his blood ("at once blood and water came out"), and Jesus' body is a site of paradox throughout the Fourth Gospel. As C. K. Barrett rightly observes, "The paradox of the [Johannine] Son of man is that even when on earth he is in heaven; . . . effectively the Son of man is in both places at once."[60] Indeed, it is because he inhabits both realms simultaneously, manifesting the unknowable otherness of God in finite flesh (cf. 1:18), that he makes communication between the two realms possible (cf. 1:51).[61] He dissolves the partition between heaven and earth, spirit and matter, figure and letter. He is not "a physical mixture, of which the elements may be separated out," so much as "a chemical compound, where the compounding elements have combined to form a new substance."[62] But he himself does not see that he is a chemical compound. Mistaking his place on the table of elements, he speaks to the Samaritan woman and all his other dialogue partners as though he were a mixture composed of separable elements, as though the living water could be clearly distinguished from spring water, the bread of life from common bread, the figurative from the literal, the spiritual from the material, and the heavenly from the earthly. What Jesus *says* is contradicted by what he *is*.

THE EROSION OF JOHANNINE IRONY

What Jesus *is*, however, is affirmed by what the Samaritan woman *says*. The distinction between the material and the spiritual was no sooner made by Jesus than it was muddied by the woman. Jesus carefully distinguished the spring water from the living water, to which she replied: "Sir, give me this water, that I may never be thirsty"—it would seem that the drachma has finally dropped—"or have to keep coming here to draw water [*mēde dierchōmai enthade antlein*]" (4:15). "The

60. C. K. Barrett, "Paradox and Dualism," in *Essays on John*, 110–11.

61. Ibid., 110, 113.

62. Ibid., 105. "Christ is the absolute hybrid," as Jean Soler has observed (quoted in John Dominic Crossan, "Difference and Divinity," *Semeia* 23 [1982]: 34).

woman has not moved with Jesus!" exclaims O'Day, echoing the response of countless other commentators. "She has understood his words in part, that his water is better than the water in Jacob's well, but she does not understand why. She interprets Jesus' words about the quenching of thirst as referring solely to physical thirst, and requests the gift of water from Jesus so that she will no longer be obliged to come to the well to draw water."[63] But can we really be sure that the water on which the woman's mind is set is material and literal only?

The exchange between Jesus and the woman is conducted under the eyes of the police. "Give me a drink," says Jesus, and the Law responds, "How is it that you, a Jew . . . ?" (4:7, 9). "From the dawn of history," notes Lacan, patriarchal culture has identified the person of the Father "with the figure of the law."[64] But there is more than one Father in this scene.

Jesus' own Father is nearby, needless to say. Jesus gestures to him in 4:23, giving expression to the Father's desire ("the Father seeks such as these to worship him"). But the woman points to a different father, or rather, to different fathers. First there is "our father Jacob, who gave us the well, and with his sons and his flocks drank from it" (4:12, RSV). Then there are "our fathers" who "worshiped on this mountain" (4:20, RSV). The woman's own identity would seem to be closely bound up with the legacy and customs of these fathers. Teresa Okure is unusually sensitive to this fact. Here is a catena of the passages in which she mentions it:

> For the woman, the well is a living testimony to her people's descent from Jacob. . . . She compares [Jesus] to Jacob, the giver of the well whose water, in her view, Jesus seems to slight. Her reply in vv 11-12 is, in effect, a defense of the ancestral water. . . . Not only does Jesus' offer of living water appear ridiculous to the woman, but as far as she is concerned, no water can be better than that of Jacob's well. . . . This is not just any well, but one that is renowned for its antiquity and whose usage goes back to the founding father himself: he, his family and all his livestock drank from it; so did generations after him. Yet despite the centuries of use, the well has neither dried up nor become exhausted. Thus, in addition to its revered ancestry,

63. O'Day, *Revelation in the Fourth Gospel*, 64.
64. Jacques Lacan, *Écrits: A Selection*, trans. Alan Sheridan (New York: Norton, 1977), 67.

the well has a character which is almost eternal. Can Jesus, then, possibily produce anything better?[65]

The woman's well water has begun to sound a good deal less like a crude dilution of Jesus' living water. "The well is deep," as she says (4:11). Blend Okure's remarks with those of Schnackenburg: "Water provides almost endless symbolism for the Oriental, to whom it appears as the most indispensable factor in life—purifying, stilling thirst, giving and renewing life and fruitfulness—which could easily be applied to the higher needs and blessings of man."[66] It begins to sound as though the water bubbling up from Jacob's well is, for the woman, more than something with which to satisfy a physical need. Indeed, it has begun to sound more and more like the water that will later flow from Jesus' side. It is not simply literal nor is it purely figurative. Another literal figure, it overflows both containers.

The reader arrives at the cross, then, only to be returned, in effect, to the well, carried by the current of a stream that flows equally between literality and figurality. As such, the narrative has forced a "sublime simplicity" on us that it led us earlier to transcend[67]—that of the woman of Samaria who desired the living water so that she might no longer have to come to the well to draw, but also that of Nicodemus perplexed that he should have to reenter his mother's womb in order to be born anew (3:4), that of the crowd who would fill their bellies with the imperishable bread (6:26-27, 34), and that of the puzzled disciples unable to distinguish plain speech from figurative (cf. 16:25, 29). In each case, two levels of meaning are collapsed that should have been kept apart. The ironic structure that positioned us on a level above these characters depended on our being able to keep the literal and figurative levels clearly separate. But the events of the death scene have collapsed the levels, disallowing their separation.

65. Okure, *The Johannine Approach to Mission*, 89, 99, 100.
66. Schnackenburg, *The Gospel According to St. John*, 1:427. Similar statements occur in Barrett, *The Gospel According to St. John*, 233, and Lightfoot, *St. John's Gospel*, 121.
67. The term "sublime simplicity," used in this way, is borrowed from Paul de Man; see *Allegories of Reading: Figural Language in Rousseau, Nietzsche, Rilke, and Proust* (New Haven, Conn.: Yale University Press, 1979), 9.

Irony—which depended on the clean separation of flesh and glory, earthly and heavenly, material and spiritual, literal and figurative, water and "water"—now collapses in paradox.[68]

In the process, that other hierarchical structure within which Jesus and the Samaritan woman conversed has also suffered some water damage. I refer, of course, to the hierarchy of male over female. If what Jesus has said to the Samaritan woman is indeed contradicted by what he is, and if what Jesus is has indeed been affirmed by what she has said, then the female student has outstripped her male teacher, even though he himself was the subject of their seminar. She has insisted, in effect, that earthly and heavenly, flesh and Spirit, figurative and literal, are symbiotically related categories: each drinks endlessly of the other, and so each is endlessly contaminated by the other. To draw a clear line between them, as Jesus attempts to do, is about as effective as drawing a line on water.[69]

GOD'S DESIRE

Earlier I argued that the flow of water from Jesus' side can be read as, among other things, a further token of the promised living water or Spirit that has now become available through Jesus' death, leaving us with a symbol (the flow of water) of a metaphor (living water) for the Spirit. But does this figurative waterslide come to a halt with the Spirit? What if the Spirit were itself a substitute for something else? Sounding uncannily Derridean, Brown defines the Johannine Paraclete as "another Jesus," "the presence of Jesus when Jesus is absent" with the Father.[70]

Tracing the water imagery upstream, therefore, we arrive at its apparent source. Contrary to what one might expect, Jesus himself

68. See Kelber, "In the Beginning Were the Words," 89. This is similar to Staley's claim that the implied reader of the Fourth Gospel is occasionally the victim of its irony (*The Print's First Kiss*, 95–118), except that in my reading it is Jesus who is the main ironic casualty.

69. This is to say that our deconstruction of the hierarchical opposition, spiritual/material, has resulted in an inversion of the hierarchical opposition, male/female (see the opening paragraph of the section "Drowning the Oppositions," p. 57). This inverted opposition could, of course, be deconstructed in its turn, should space permit it or strategy require it.

70. Brown, *The Gospel According to John (XIII–XXI)*, 1141.

is not that source. The stream does not issue from Jesus' presence; rather, it is from Jesus' absence that it flows. The time in which the Fourth Evangelist is writing is the time of the Paraclete (cf. 14:26; 15:26; 16:7-15; 20:22-23), a time when Jesus is away with the Father. And absence is the source of desire. Schnackenburg remarks: "The figurative expression ['living water'] on the lips of Jesus can have become for the evangelist a symbol of all that Jesus meant to him." And in using this symbol he may also have been taking into account the "religious desires of his readers."[71] The water imagery in John is a river of desire, then; it issues from the Fourth Evangelist, although it cannot be said to have originated with him.

But neither can this river of desire be said to empty into Jesus. For Jesus too is driven by desire, carried along in its current, until he reunites with his Father in death, as a river reunites with the sea from which it sprang. The Father is the ultimate object of Jesus' desire in the Fourth Gospel. But even the Father is not free of desire; it was to accomplish the Father's *thelēma* (will, wish, desire) that the Son was sent into the world (4:34; 5:30; 6:38; 7:16; 8:28, 42; 12:49; 14:10, 24; 15:10; 17:4). And so the sea into which the river finally empties itself is a chasm hollowed out by desire—the Father's desire to be the desire of the Son and those whom he draws to himself through the Son (6:44, 65; cf. 12:32; 17:20-26). As Lacan has suggested, what distinguishes both the Jewish and Christian traditions from most Asian religious traditions is that the former turn not on God's bliss, but on God's desire.[72] God's desire is a black hole that slowly draws the Johannine cosmos into it.[73]

For many who have written on the scene at the Samaritan well, the woman's oblivion to her own need, assumed to be so much

71. Schnackenburg, *The Gospel According to St. John*, 1:427.

72. Jacques Lacan, "Introduction to the Names-of-the-Father Seminar," translated by Jeffrey Mehlman, in *Television/A Challenge to the Psychoanalytic Establishment* (New York: Norton, 1990), 89–90; cf. idem, *Le Séminaire, livre III: Les Psychoses*, ed. Jacques-Alain Miller (Paris: Seuil, 1981), 323ff.

73. This would be my reply to Hendrikus Boers, apropos of the Fourth Gospel, when he writes: "It has always been my interest to discover a kind of metaphysics of New Testament texts. I want to know what holds the text together from its inside" (*Neither on This Mountain Nor in Jerusalem: A Study of John 4* [Atlanta: Scholars Press, 1988], xv).

greater than that of Jesus, is the pivot on which the irony of their dialogue turns. Deeper by far, however, is the irony that Jesus' own need—not to mention that of his Father—is just as great as the woman's. "The well is deep," as the woman says; desire, however, is bottomless.

3

HOW DECONSTRUCTION DIFFERS FROM SOURCE- AND STORY-CENTERED GOSPEL STUDIES

GAIL O'DAY'S *Revelation in the Fourth Gospel* has a literary reading of John 4:4-42 as its centerpiece. She writes: "It is . . . my working assumption that John 4:4-42 is an intentional literary unity, a composition that can and should be examined and interpreted in its final form." She adds: "This is not to deny the complexities of the text nor the author's possible use of sources." Nevertheless, "[t]he meaning and interpretation of the text are not to be derived from its prehistory, but from its final form."[1]

O'Day's statement is typical of the new literary criticism of the Gospels—*narrative criticism*, as it has come to be called.[2] No less representative is the following complaint from R. Alan Culpepper's *Anatomy of the Fourth Gospel*: "Johannine scholars have generally approached the text looking for tensions, inconsistencies, or 'aporias' which suggest that separate strains or layers of material are present in the text." In consequence, "little attention has been given to the integrity of the whole, the ways its component parts interrelate, its

---

1. O'Day, *Revelation in the Fourth Gospel*, 50.
2. See Glossary, and see further Mark Allan Powell, *What Is Narrative Criticism?* (Minneapolis: Fortress Press, 1990), and Stephen D. Moore, *Literary Criticism and the Gospels* (New Haven, Conn.: Yale University Press, 1989), 1–68.

effects upon the reader, or the way it achieves its effects."[3] Rudolf Bultmann's classic commentary on John contains a brief section on "The Integrity of the Gospel" that contrasts interestingly with such claims and complaints. The Fourth Gospel in its canonical form has no integrity for Bultmann. Where O'Day, Culpepper, and other narrative critics detect tidiness and order, Bultmann sees only an unmade bed littered with loose sheets of a lost manuscript:

> The thesis has been represented, occasionally even in very early times but strongly from the beginning of this century, that the original order of the text has been disturbed, through an interchange of leaves or by some other means. For example Jn. 6.1 reports a journey of Jesus to the other bank of Lake Gennesaret, although chapter 5 is set in Jerusalem: 7.15-24 harks back directly to the sabbath healing that lies far off in chapter 5. 14.30f. leads on directly to the Passion story in ch. 18, while the discourse continues in chapter 15. From these and many other examples it must be presumed that the present order of our Gospel is not derived from the author. . . . How the present (lack of) order came about cannot be determined with certainty. . . . The assumption lies closest to hand that the Gospel of John was edited from the author's literary remains on the basis of separate manuscript pages, left without order.[4]

A literary remains covered with unidentified fingerprints, a clumsily altered will ("there are reasons for doubting whether the Gospel itself has found entrance into the ecclesiastical tradition in the form intended by the author")[5]—these are tantalizing clues that pose an irresistible challenge for the scholar-sleuth. Can he or she reconstruct the sequence of events that resulted in this mutilated literary corpus?

DECONSTRUCTION'S ELDERLY UNCLE

Such sleuthing, moreover—the quest for sources, coupled with the investigation of the alterations, disguises, and plastic surgeries that they have undergone—was termed *literary criticism* under the old dispensation. Consider the way the term is used by Bultmann's distinguished pupil Hans Conzelmann, for example. Conzelmann teamed up with a student of his own, Andreas Lindemann, to produce an

---

3. Culpepper, *Anatomy of the Fourth Gospel*, 3.
4. Bultmann, *The Gospel of John*, 10–11.
5. Ibid., 10.

ambitious *Arbeitsbuch zum Neuen Testament* (New Testament Workbook).[6] Their principal section on the Fourth Gospel is entitled "Sources and other literary-critical issues."[7] And in their chapter on the Synoptic Gospels we read: "Literary criticism does not examine the individual passages of tradition; rather, it evaluates the different traditions in Matthew, Mark, and Luke *in their relationship* to one another, notwithstanding the importance of placing a paragraph (pericope), alongside its actual message, within the structure of the gospel."[8] But since the characteristic gesture of the new literary criticism of the Gospels is precisely that of situating each passage within the overall structure (plot) of the Gospel in which it is found, its exact relationship to parallel passages in the other Gospels (if any) sharply reducing in importance, it would appear that the new literary criticism represents a direct reversal of the priorities of the old literary criticism. The backdrop has been wheeled into the foreground, and what was once the foreground has become the backdrop.

Elsewhere I have argued that narrative criticism, the most widely disseminated variety of the new literary criticism, far from being simply another method plucked from the broad field of "secular" literary studies (more and more a field without fences), is instead a hothouse hybrid, the result of a peculiar series of grafts.[9] For there is no shrub by that name in the secular field, and nothing with its exact physiology. It is rooted in redaction criticism, which also forms its trunk. Onto this trunk some theoretical shoots cut from secular narratology have been grafted—a conception of the literary text as a communication between an author and a reader conducted through a set of intermediary personae (implied author, narrator, narratee, and implied reader), joined to a conception of the narrative text as an

---

6. Hans Conzelmann and Andreas Lindemann, *Arbeitsbuch zum Neuen Testament* (Tübingen: J. C. B. Mohr [Paul Siebeck], 1975); trans. Siegfried S. Schatzmann, as *Interpreting the New Testament: An Introduction to the Principles and Methods of N.T. Exegesis* (Peabody, Mass.: Hendrickson, 1988).

7. Conzelmann and Lindemann, *Interpreting the New Testament*, 248–52. Compare Schnackenburg's "Literary Criticism of the Gospel of St. John" in his *Gospel According to St. John*, 1:44–58.

8. Conzelmann and Lindemann, *Interpreting the New Testament*, 46, their emphasis.

9. Moore, *Literary Criticism and the Gospels*, esp. 51–55.

autonomous story world whose basic elements are plot, characters, and settings, and to a preoccupation with the rhetorical techniques used by the author to transmit the story to the reader.

Harder to account for as a simple cutting from current literary theory is narrative's criticism's passion for arguing the unity of the biblical narratives,[10] a passion that has led many biblical scholars to assume that secular literary studies is a discipline preoccupied with the unity of literary texts—an impression well wide of the mark, except in the sense that textual unity has been one of its most contested concepts in recent decades. To find a close secular analogue for narrative criticism's penchant for holistic reading we must go all the way back to the 1930s and 1940s, the golden age of the New Criticism, a movement for which the literary work of art, preeminently the poem, was an autonomous, internally unified organism, the bearer of a meaning that had to be validated first and foremost by the context of the work itself, as opposed to its historical setting. To oversimplify a little, as the New Criticism was to American literary criticism of the 1930s, 1940s, and 1950s, so has poststructuralism (deconstruction and its siblings) been to American literary criticism of the 1970s and 1980s, which is to say the reigning paradigm, insofar as there has been one during this turbulent period.[11]

Strange to say, deconstruction appears to have less in common with the new literary criticism of the Gospels than with the old. Back in the dark ages of Gospel studies, scholars would subject the text to stringent scrutiny, "looking for tensions, inconsistencies, or 'aporias,'" as Culpepper remarks.[12] Indeed, such inquisitions are not unknown today, even in North American biblical scholarship. Culpepper's use

10. For a prime example, see Robert C. Tannehill, *The Narrative Unity of Luke-Acts: A Literary Interpretation* (2 vols.; Philadelphia and Minneapolis: Fortress Press, 1986–90). Many more examples are listed in Powell, *What Is Narrative Criticism?* and Moore, *Literary Criticism and the Gospels.*

11. The 1980s was also the decade when academic feminism came into its own, and when two new interdisciplinary fields made their appearance: gender studies and cultural studies. All three areas intersect with poststructuralism in complex ways. Another 1980s arrival, the New Historicism, was more directly indebted to poststructuralism. On gender studies, see "Introduction," n. 11; on cultural studies, see Lawrence Grossberg, Cary Nelson, and Paul A. Treichler, eds., *Cultural Studies* (New York: Routledge, 1992); and on New Historicism, see Further Reading.

12. Culpepper, *Anatomy of the Fourth Gospel,* 3.

of the term *aporia* here is intriguing; it is a term that crops up regularly both in Gospel scholarship and deconstructive criticism. It is a term especially frequent in Johannine studies.

Robert T. Fortna is one Johannine scholar who is unfashionable enough to feel for aporias as he reads. Fortna defines aporias as "the roughnesses and tensions—the interruptions and sudden turns, non sequiturs and even contradictions, passages with dense or overloaded wording, the doublets—that so patently characterize 4G [the Fourth Gospel] and distinguish it from the narratives of the other Gospels."[13] For an example of "this textual tension," Fortna directs us to John 4:48, where, in the midst of "a simple, straightforward miracle story like so many in the Gospels," Jesus exclaims, "Unless you people see signs and wonders, you refuse to believe!"—a cruel outburst, according to my more irreverent undergraduates; an illogical one, according to Fortna:

> The official had not asked for a sign, still less demanded to believe; certainly he believed in some fashion already. So why Jesus' outburst . . . ? Whom is Jesus addressing? Why does he use the second-person plural in speaking . . . to an individual? And most puzzling of all, why after his reluctance to be a miracle-worker does Jesus proceed to grant the official's request, and specifically to work a "sign" (v. 54), a term treated so polemically in v. 48? Unless we go to extraordinary lengths to vindicate the passage as smooth and consistent, such questions force us to doubt the passage's integrity.[14]

At such points, deconstruction yawns comfortably, stretches out on the couch, and snuggles up to its aged relative, the old literary criticism of the Gospels. For deconstruction too entails "scrupulous attention to what seems ancillary or resistant to understanding" in a text, as Paul de Man puts it, and is suspicious, in dealing with earlier readings, of attempts to blur, conceal, or circumvent whatever stands

---

13. Robert Tomson Fortna, *The Fourth Gospel and Its Predecessor* (Philadelphia: Fortress Press, 1988), 4. The Synoptics do also "contain a few aporias," he admits (ibid., n. 7). Fortna's earlier book, *The Gospel of Signs: A Reconstruction of the Narrative Source Underlying the Fourth Gospel* (Cambridge: Cambridge University Press, 1970), also begins with a discussion of aporias (2–8). There he credits Eduard Schwartz with first applying the term to the Johannine material in 1907 (2 n. 3).

14. Fortna, *The Fourth Gospel and Its Predecessor*, 5.

in the way of coherence.[15] (Fortna is similarly wary of recent attempts to "overassert" the unity of the Fourth Gospel.)[16] "What would happen," asks de Man, "if, for once, one were to reverse the ethos of explication"—explication at any cost, that is—"and try to be really precise," to examine every resistance to meaning that the text throws in our path?[17]

Such resistances de Man termed *aporias* on occasion—points at which the reader's path (*poros*) becomes impassable (*aporos*) or impossible.[18] The most explicit statement on the role of aporias in deconstruction, however, comes from J. Hillis Miller, who once remarked of de Man and Derrida:

> These critics are not tragic or Dionysian in the sense that their work is wildly orgiastic or irrational. No critic could be more rigorously sane and rational, Apollonian, in his procedure, for example, than Paul de Man. One feature of Derrida's criticism is a patient and minutely philological "explication de texte." Nevertheless, the thread of logic leads in both cases into regions which are alogical, absurd. . . . *Sooner or later there is an encounter with an "aporia" or impasse.* . . . In fact the moment when logic fails in their work is the moment of their deepest penetration into the actual nature of literary language, or of language as such.[19]

Similarly for the older literary criticism of the Gospels, the aporia enables deep penetration into the nature of Gospel literature. "[T]he aporias provide us the means to a fuller understanding of the document containing them," says Fortna.[20] Recall the example given earlier, Jesus' incomprehensible outburst in the midst of "a simple, straightforward miracle story." The "most natural explanation" of this embarrassing outburst, for Fortna, is that it is an editorial insertion; "the narrative stems from more than one author: it consists of an older

15. Paul de Man, "Foreword to Carol Jacobs, *The Dissimulating Harmony*," in *Critical Writings, 1953–1978*, ed. Lindsay Waters (Minneapolis: University of Minnesota Press, 1989), 220.

16. Fortna, *The Fourth Gospel and its Predecessor*, 8 n. 19.

17. De Man, "Foreword," 220.

18. For a notable example of such usage, see de Man, *Allegories of Reading*, 131.

19. J. Hillis Miller, "Stevens' Rock and Criticism as Cure, II," *Georgia Review* 30 (1976): 338, emphasis added.

20. Fortna, *The Fourth Gospel and Its Predecessor*, 9.

and a younger layer."[21] In other words, the petulant Jesus of 4:48 is younger than the Jesus of the source narrative that the Johannine author was using; "[t]he aporias show us just where the source is laid aside and taken up again."[22]

For Fortna, the aporias are an accidental feature of the Fourth Gospel; they "are just those points at which a more thorough recasting of the source(s) would have produced a smoother present text without aporias."[23] And again: "The aporias such as we find in 4G [the Fourth Gospel], and only there, are the result of the thorough yet respectful redaction that 4E [the Fourth Evangelist] has done on the source; a more radical rewriting (e.g., as Matthew and Luke rewrite Mark) would have evened out roughnesses of this sort, leaving a far smoother text—without aporias."[24] A more radical rewriting—or a more radical re-reading: the new literary criticism of 4G would seem to have picked up 4E's discarded plane, intent on evening out these residual rough-nesses. Fernando F. Segovia, introducing a recent collection of such readings, suggests that considerable progress has been made in this task: "[T]he more any text is shown to be meaningful and coherent as it stands, the more difficult it becomes to accept the presence of aporias as traditionally conceived and defined."[25]

At this point, deconstruction abruptly disengages itself from the embrace of its aged relative, the old literary criticism of the Gospels, leaving the latter to discover that it still has something in common after all with its estranged offspring, the new literary criticism of the Gospels: both believe in the avoidability of aporias. For Derrida and de Man, in contrast, aporias are not accidental features of the text, unhappy contingencies that could have been avoided had the author been more careful, or more skillful, or had a more efficient plane with which to even out the roughnesses of the narrative (had 4E had access to a PC, for example). Indeed, de Man was especially drawn to texts

21. Ibid., 5.
22. Ibid., 9. Cf. ibid, 61–65, and *The Gospel of Signs*, 38–48, for Fortna's detailed analyses of this pericope.
23. Fortna, *The Fourth Gospel and Its Predecessor*, 6. Cf. Fortna, *The Gospel of Signs*, 3.
24. Fortna, *The Fourth Gospel and Its Predecessor*, 7.
25. Fernando F. Segovia, "Towards a New Direction in Johannine Scholarship: The Fourth Gospel from a Literary Perspective," *Semeia* 53 (1991): 14. Segovia's subtitle is also the title of this issue of *Semeia*.

that initially felt smooth to the touch. Introducing *Allegories of Reading*, for example, he explains that his inclusion of Proust and Rilke among the writers with whom he will deal is dictated in part by their stubborn resistance to his way of reading: "[O]ne could argue that if *their* work yields to such [readings], the same would necessarily be true for writers whose rhetorical strategies are less hidden"[26]—John, for example?

Clearly, "aporia" does not have quite the same meaning for deconstructors as for Fortna and other source critics of the Bible. My *Webster's* gives a double definition of the term: "1: a problem or difficulty arising from an awareness of opposing or incompatible views on the same theoretic matter; *esp*: one giving rise to philosophically systematic doubt. 2: a passage in speech or writing incorporating or presenting a difficulty or doubt." The first definition is closest to a deconstructive understanding of aporia, one bound up with explicit theories of language, while the second is closest to the biblical scholarly understanding of the term, one bound up with implicit (commonsensical) theories of language. As we have seen, Derridean deconstruction ascribes considerable significance to the aporetic elements in language that Derrida terms "undecidables," elements "that can no longer be included within philosophical (binary) opposition, but which, however, inhabit philosophical opposition, resisting and disorganizing it, *without ever* constituting a third term, without ever leaving room for a solution in the form of speculative dialectics."[27]

Similarly for de Man, reading repeatedly confronts us with an aporetic "residue of meaning that remains beyond the reach of the text's own logic."[28] (The water that issues from the Johannine Jesus' side would be one such residue.) Typically, for de Man, the text will compel us to choose between two options "while destroying the foundations of any choice," each option being "precisely the error denounced by the other."[29] (Such is the situation with regard to literal and figurative language in the Fourth Gospel, as we saw.)

26. De Man, *Allegories of Reading*, ix.
27. Derrida, *Positions*, 43, his emphasis.
28. De Man, *Allegories of Reading*, 99.
29. Ibid., 245, 12. For an elaboration of the subtle differences between Derrida's concept of "undecidability" and de Man's concept of "unreadability," see Jeffrey T. Nealon, "The Discipline of Deconstruction," *PMLA* 107 (1992): 1266–79.

What is actually at stake in this deconstructive obsession with aporias? One thing that is at stake, arguably, is critical authority itself: the pretensions of one form of discourse (criticism) to speak authoritatively on behalf of another (literature). What if both these modes of discourse were hopelessly entangled to begin with, critical language every bit as snarled in rhetorical tropes as literary language? Criticism sets out to subjugate literary language, conscripting language in order to do so; small wonder if language revolts. In the course of this uncivil war, curious knots and contradictions—aporias—come about. These knots, nets, and traps have been a source of particular fascination for deconstruction. At issue, too, in this tussle are the limitations of critical method. Criticism's desire to be fully in control is nowhere more evident than in its addiction to method; among other things, deconstruction is a "methodone" clinic, designed to loosen the grip of that addiction. All of this is very far from the old literary criticism of the Gospels.

Of course, deconstructive literary criticism, especially the "Yale school" of de Man, Miller & Co., is itself old, so old indeed as to be dead, if the obituary columns in the journals are to be believed.[30] Moreover, it is the Yale brand of deconstruction that is particularly associated with the quest for quirks and quarks—aporias and other oddities—in literature. As is now generally agreed, the problem with Yale deconstruction and the vast critical industry that it spawned was that the pinpointing of aporias in literary texts all too often became an end in itself, to the neglect of other more concrete aporias or impasses facing many literary scholars and their students (not to mention innumerable others with no direct stake in literature), especially if they happened to be female, or persons of color, or both. "[T]he Yale school has always been a Male School," Barbara Johnson announced in 1984,[31] around the time that she began to divert her own efforts from de Man-powered readings of literary texts into singularly

---

30. The opening of Nealon's article is a typical example: "Deconstruction, it seems, is dead in literature departments today. While plenty of discourse is still produced concerning deconstruction, its heyday has apparently passed" ("The Discipline of Deconstruction," 1266).

31. Barbara Johnson, "Gender Theory and the Yale School," in *A World of Difference*, 32. Johnson herself was a "junior member" of that school. Her earlier book, *The Critical Difference: Essays in the Contemporary Rhetoric of Reading* (Baltimore: Johns Hopkins University Press, 1980), remains an outstanding example of Yale deconstruction in its prepolitical phase.

un-de Manian areas of inquiry, such as those of gender and race.[32] And that, generally speaking, is where deconstruction is still at today, if it is anywhere; in part it has been swept away, in part swept up, in the widespread politicization of American literary studies that has been under way since at least the early 1980s.

OUR TEXTS ARE NO MORE UNIFIED THAN WE ARE

The unconscious is that chapter of my history that is marked by a blank or occupied by a falsehood: it is the censored chapter.

—*Jacques Lacan*[33]

What of deconstruction's relationship to the new literary criticism of the Gospels? Recall the statements by Culpepper and O'Day with which this chapter began. In my own reading of the Fourth Gospel I have, like Culpepper, attended to the complex ways in which the component parts of the text interrelate, and to the interaction between text and reader. Like O'Day, I have attended to the irony flowing between Jesus, the Samaritan woman, and the reader. And like both of them, I have focused my energies on the "final form" of the text.

In contrast to Culpepper and O'Day, however, my "working assumption" as I read the Fourth Gospel was *not* that it is "an intentional literary unity," a composition successfully unified by an author's governing intention, a well-integrated whole.[34] Instead I expected the tensions, inconsistencies, and aporias that Culpepper relegates to the older paradigm to resurface—although not necessarily, or at least not only, because of "separate strains or layers of material [that] are present in the text."[35] My reading of the water discourse drifted into areas where the ability of the narrative to achieve its ostensible aim of leading the audience through complications and deferrals to a climactic, completed understanding—the ability that narrative criticism celebrates—

32. See especially the later essays in Johnson's *A World of Difference.* Other younger critics who began to push Yale deconstruction in new directions included Michael Ryan and Gayatri Chakravorty Spivak. See Michael Ryan, *Marxism and Deconstruction: A Critical Articulation* (Baltimore: Johns Hopkins University Press, 1982), and Spivak, *In Other Worlds.*

33. Lacan, *Écrits*, 50.

34. See O'Day, *Revelation in the Fourth Gospel*, 50.

35. Culpepper, *Anatomy of the Fourth Gospel*, 3.

foundered and went under. Was this what the Johannine author[36] had in mind as he constructed a discourse (up)on water? Hardly, but here I have been as interested in what might be said to be out of the control of this author as in anything that might be said to be within his control. And whereas much that is recognizably Johannine has undoubtedly resurfaced in my reading, I seem to have also dredged up in addition "a yet quite unformed mass of roots, soil, and sediments."[37]

At issue, ultimately, in these different working assumptions are different philosophies of human identity. Norman N. Holland, a psychoanalytic literary critic best known as a pioneer of reader-response criticism, once proposed an intriguing homology: "*Unity* is to *text* as *identity* is to *self*."[38] While I am persuaded by Holland's homology, I find his understanding of identity less convincing. For Holland, identity is "an unchanging essence . . . that permeates the millions of ego choices" that constitute each human self.[39] Of course, Holland was not the first to propose that there is an unchanging essence within each of us. Plato, for one, beat him to it,[40] although Plato termed this essence the soul, as did Augustine and numerous other Neoplatonic theologians. All of which suggests that Holland's concept of identity is yet another theological notion that has gone underground only to reemerge in secular guise.

Nearer to hand, Holland's concept of identity is plucked from that branch of the Freudian tree commonly known as *ego psychology*, a highly successful, thoroughly pragmatic, and distinctively American version of the talking cure. For the founders of ego psychology (notably, Ernst Kris, Erik Erikson, Heinz Hartmann, and Rudolph Loewenstein),[41] psychoanalysis was first and foremost a therapeutic technique designed to help disturbed individuals better adapt to society. For them,

36. For simplicity's sake, let us speak as though he (she?) were one.
37. Derrida, *Of Grammatology*, 161. Cf. 157–64, all highly relevant to the present discussion.
38. Norman N. Holland, "Unity Identity Text Self," in *Reader-Response Criticism: From Formalism to Post-Structuralism*, ed. Jane P. Tompkins (Baltimore: Johns Hopkins University Press, 1980), 121, his emphasis.
39. Ibid.
40. Holland himself is not unaware of this; he appeals to Aristotle, for example, in arguing his case (ibid., 121–22).
41. In his essay, Holland draws on the work of another influential ego psychologist, Heinz Lichtenstein.

the ego was the principle of unity and identity in the human subject, the integrative force that holds everything together by maintaining a delicate balance between internal demands and external prohibitions. The ego mediates between the claims of the id, on the one hand, and those of external reality, on the other. A robust ego is therefore the goal of psychoanalysis.[42]

What other goal could psychoanalysis possibly have? This brings us to Lacan, who, as it happens, was himself analyzed by Rudolph Loewenstein before the latter emigrated to the United States. Here is how Lacan's biographer, Elisabeth Roudinesco, contrasts the two:

> In Loewenstein's eyes, psychoanalysis was first of all a medical method for curing symptoms and understanding resistances, whereas for Lacan, it was above all an intellectual epic, a discovery of the mind, a theoretical journey. Thus the therapy of the young psychiatrist by the future founder of "ego psychology" [in 1932] already bore within it the seeds of the conflict that would break out twenty years later and would oppose, on the one hand, the defenders of a psychoanalysis tending to see itself as a therapeutic . . . technique, and, on the other, the partisans of a philosophical adventure that might renew the great message from Vienna.[43]

To put it all too crudely, whereas the ego psychologists took their lead from an optimistic reading of Freud's *The Ego and the Id*, in particular its characterization of psychoanalysis as "an instrument to enable the ego to achieve a progressive conquest of the id,"[44] Lacan took his lead from a pessimistic reading of Freud's earlier works, which highlight the subversive operations of the unconscious.[45] Lacan holds Freud to

42. For more on ego psychology and Holland's relationship to it, see Elizabeth Wright, *Psychoanalytic Criticism: Theory in Practice* (2d ed.; New York: Methuen, 1987), 56–68.

43. Elisabeth Roudinesco, *Jacques Lacan & Co.: A History of Psychoanalysis in France, 1925–1985*, trans. Jeffrey Mehlman (Chicago: University of Chicago Press, 1990), 119.

44. Sigmund Freud, *The Ego and the Id*, in *The Standard Edition of the Complete Psychological Works of Sigmund Freud*, ed. and trans. James Strachey (London: Hogarth Press, 1953–74), 19:56.

45. Foremost among these works, for Lacan, are *The Interpretation of Dreams* (*Standard Edition*, vols. 4–5), *The Psychopathology of Everyday Life* (vol. 6), and *Jokes and Their Relation to the Unconscious* (vol. 8); see Lacan, *Écrits*, 170.

his unsettling early vision of the human subject as split or profoundly disunified, even to the point of accusing the later Freud of backing away from his early insights.

More especially, Lacan accused ego psychology, and the psychoanalytic establishment in general, not to mention popular psychotherapy, of having rendered Freud's revolutionary discovery banal.[46] For the essence of that discovery, as Lacan reads it, is not so much that the unconscious exists as that it "speaks" (indeed, it cannot be silenced), that its discourse is the locus of truth for each subject (it harbors the subject's unconscious desires), and that all conscious discourse is therefore but a dim refraction of unconscious truth. The latter can only reveal itself through dreams, slips of the tongue or pen, purposeful forgetting, bungled actions, and other indirect means. "All I can do is tell the truth," says Lacan, immediately adding, "No, that isn't so—I have missed it. There is no truth that, in passing through awareness, does not lie. But one runs after it all the same."[47]

In Saussurean terms—and Lacan was an avid reader of Saussure—what Freud discovered is that a fissure opens up between the signified (unconscious desire) and the signifier (desire's alienated expression in conscious speech and action), and that every conception of a unified human subject necessarily slides into that fissure. For Lacan, ego psychology and its popular variant, psychotherapy, seek "to return psychoanalysis to a pre-Freudian state,"[48] one in which the ego, as a principle of unity, continuity, and identity, is the force that controls the psyche. "The radical heteronomy that Freud's discovery shows gaping within man," objects Lacan, "can never again be covered over without whatever is used to hide it being profoundly dishonest."[49]

The first thing that hides this heterogeneity or disunity is the mirror. Lacan locates the mirror stage somewhere between the ages of six and eighteen months. Still in a state of relative motor

46. Cf. Ellie Ragland-Sullivan, *Jacques Lacan and the Philosophy of Psychoanalysis* (Urbana and Chicago: University of Illinois Press, 1986), 119.

47. Jacques Lacan, *The Four Fundamental Concepts of Psycho-Analysis*, ed. Jacques-Alain Miller, trans. Alan Sheridan (New York: Norton, 1978), vii.

48. Jane Gallop, *Reading Lacan* (Ithaca, N.Y.: Cornell University Press, 1985), 98.

49. Lacan, *Écrits*, 172; cf. 165–66.

incoordination, the child sees her image in a mirror (not an actual mirror, necessarily—it could simply be the image of herself that she receives back from her primary care giver). Henceforth the child will attempt to assume this image, to mimic it, to model herself upon it, because the image appears to possess the coherence that the child herself lacks. (Prior to the mirror stage, the infant experiences itself as a "body in fragments," according to Lacan, an amorphous mass of sensations and impressions, with no clearly conceived bodily boundaries.) The real import of the mirror stage, for Lacan, is that individual identity is founded upon a fiction, a misrecognition, a division, and that the introjection of the mirror image sets the stage for a life of alienation. For like the mirror-stage infant, the adult subject will be able to experience itself *as* a self only through images that come to it from outside, to see its self only as others see it or not to see its self at all.[50]

Biblical criticism is at present passing through a mirror stage. An intriguing symptom of this passage crops up in Culpepper's *Anatomy*. Like other narrative critics before him,[51] Culpepper appeals to Murray Krieger's metaphors of the text as window and the text as mirror.[52] "[I]t is clear that John has been used as a 'window,' " writes Culpepper, "through which the critic can catch 'glimpses' of the history of the Johannine community. The meaning of the gospel derives from the way it was related to that history. The meaning of the text, therefore, is assumed to lie on the other side of the window."[53] What might it

50. For Lacan's own (difficult) account of the mirror stage, see *Écrits*, 1–7. For a more thorough unpacking of this account, see Malcolm Bowie, *Lacan* (Cambridge, Mass.: Harvard University Press, 1991), 21–26.

51. Notably Norman R. Petersen; see his *Literary Criticism for New Testament Critics* (Philadelphia: Fortress Press, 1978), 19.

52. Culpepper, *Anatomy of the Fourth Gospel*, 3–5. Cf. Murray Krieger, *A Window to Criticism: Shakespeare's Sonnets and Modern Poetics* (Princeton, N.J.: Princeton University Press, 1964), 3-4. The present reflections were sparked, however, not by Culpepper's application of the mirror metaphor to John, but by Elizabeth Struthers Malbon's application of it to Mark in "Text and Contexts: Interpreting the Disciples in Mark." Malbon's article is forthcoming in *Semeia*, as is my own response to it, on which the present discussion is based. I've switched from Malbon to Culpepper here in order to keep the discussion focused on John, but also because I find *Anatomy of the Fourth Gospel* to be even more provocative from a Lacanian perspective.

53. Culpepper, *Anatomy of the Fourth Gospel*, 3.

mean to view the text as a mirror? "This model assumes that the meaning of the text lies on this side of it," explains Culpepper, "between mirror and observer, text and reader."[54] Using the mirror model, "readers may be helped to read the gospel more perceptively by *looking at* certain features of the gospel. This process is to be distinguished from reading the gospel *looking for* particular kinds of historical evidence."[55]

Of course, when the reader looks at the text as a mirror, peers into it, he or she can expect to see his or her own eye in reflection. I confess that I was somewhat startled, then, to turn to the next page of the *Anatomy* and find an outsized eye staring back at me:[56]

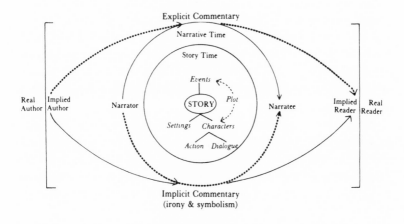

The message insistently writing itself on the mirror of Culpepper's own text would seem, to me at least, to be this: when the interpreter looks at the Gospel text as a mirror, he or she also necessarily sees himself or herself (for a mirror has no image proper to itself, being the emptiest of blank surfaces). And it naturally follows that the more unity and

54. Ibid., 4.
55. Ibid., 5, his emphasis.
56. Ibid., 6. This is Culpepper's modified version of Seymour Chatman's (rectangular, altogether unoptical) diagram of narrative communication. See Seymour Chatman, *Story and Discourse: Narrative Structure in Fiction and Film* (Ithaca, N.Y.: Cornell University Press, 1978), 267.

coherence the interpreter is able to ascribe to the text, the more reassuring and confirming will be the self-reflection he or she receives
back from it.

It is not only in its preoccupation with narrative coherence,
however, that current literary criticism of the Gospels shows itself to
be trapped in a hall of mirrors. Reader-response criticism is also per-
formed in front of a mirror. Culpepper writes: "The narrator conveys
the author's perspective to the reader and sends signals which establish
expectations, distance and intimacy, and powerfully affect the reader's
sense of identification and involvement."[57] To read as a reader-response
critic reads is to attempt to assume the image of the reader envisioned
by the author and projected by the text, to mimic this image, to model
your reading upon it, because the image possesses certain desirable
qualities that you, as a critic, lack, such as innocence of what comes
next in the plot and hence an ability to be affected by it. (Prior to the
mirror stage, the biblical critic experienced the text as a "body in
fragments," a heterogeneous mass of materials possessing little overall
coherence, and as such projecting no single, unified role that the critic
could assume and introject.)

As Jane Gallop rightly remarks, "Lacan's writings contain an
implicit ethical imperative to break the mirror."[58] The imperative is
also an epistemological one, for it is urged in the name of truth. And
if I am personally disposed to submit to this "imperative," it is because
I strongly suspect that in the last analysis—indeed, after the last analysis—our texts are no more unified than we ourselves are.

The family resemblance between Lacanian psychoanalysis and
Derridean deconstruction is, of course, striking.[59] Central to each is a
necessary inability, the inability to dominate the text (for Lacan, the
psyche is a kind of "text"),[60] to unify and center it through a reading

57. Culpepper, *Anatomy of the Fourth Gospel*, 4. Cf. 205–211,
which explains how the text fashions the reader's "identity."

58. Gallop, *Reading Lacan*, 59. More enigmatically, "the charge is
to look into the mirror and see not the image but the mirror itself" (62).

59. Notwithstanding Derrida's stern critique of Lacan. See Jacques
Derrida, "Le Facteur de la vérité" (in English, despite the title), in *The Post
Card*, 411–96.

60. More precisely, a kind of language, one with profound similarities
to literary language. For Lacan's clearest statement on this, see "Of Structure
as an Inmixing of an Otherness Prerequisite to Any Subject Whatever," in *The*

that would harmonize or "totalize" everything that is going on in it. Like deconstruction, moreover, and unlike psychotherapy, Lacanian analysis "does not provoke any triumph of self-awareness. . . . It uncovers, on the contrary, a process of decentering, in which the subject delves . . . into the loss of his mastery." [61]

I readily concede, however, that if the idea of a unified identity, corresponding to the idea of a unified text (recall Holland's homology), is a displaced theological idea descended from the ancient and medieval concept of the soul, the opposite idea of a split or fragmented subject, corresponding to a fragmented text, is an idea itself no less theological. The theological repressed continues to return in ever more unlikely guises. "Lacan's major statement of ethical purpose and therapeutic goal," notes Gallop, "is that one must accept one's castration"[62]—even, or especially, if one is male. Castration is primarily a linguistic affair for Lacan: "[W]e are inevitably bereft of any masterful understanding of language, and can only signify ourselves in a symbolic system that we do not command, that, rather, commands us."[63]

What is most striking for me, however, about "Lacan's major statement of ethical purpose and therapeutic goal" is the fact that it smacks so strongly of the doctrine of original sin. Indeed, Lacan himself was capable of such lapsarian pronouncements as: "[F]orever, by dint of a central fault, desire is separated from fulfillment"; or again: "[psychoanalysis] is engaged in the central lack in which the subject experiences himself as desire."[64] Is it my own strict Roman Catholic upbringing that renders these austere ideas so attractive to me?

Structuralist Controversy: The Languages of Criticism and the Sciences of Man, ed. Richard Macksey and Eugenio Donato (Baltimore: Johns Hopkins University Press, 1970), 187.

61. Roudinesco, *Jacques Lacan & Co.*, 255.

62. Gallop, *Reading Lacan*, 20.

63. Ibid. Gallop adds: "For women, Lacan's message that everyone, regardless of his or her organs, is 'castrated,' represents not a loss but a gain." For more on Lacan and feminism, see Elizabeth Grosz, *Jacques Lacan: A Feminist Introduction* (New York: Routledge, 1990).

64. Lacan, "Introduction to the Names-of-the-Father Seminar," 86, and *Four Fundamental Concepts of Psycho-Analysis*, 265.

PART TWO
FOUCAULT

4
FOUCAULT FROM
INSANITY TO CHRISTIANITY

> The work of the intellect is to show that what is, does not have to be what it is.
>
> —*Michel Foucault*[1]

A WELL-WORN topic of Foucault commentary is the question of when precisely structuralist Foucault expired (assuming he ever really existed) and poststructuralist Foucault was born. The answer usually ventured runs along the following lines: Up to and including his 1969 book, *The Archaeology of Knowledge*, Foucault's work has a faintly structuralist feel; after the *Archaeology*, this feel begins to fade.[2]

"STRUCTURALIST" FOUCAULT

Along with Claude Lévi-Strauss, Jacques Lacan, Louis Althusser, and Roland Barthes, Foucault was once thought to be a cardinal representative of structuralism, if not the pontiff himself. Foucault was anything

1. Foucault, "How Much Does It Cost for Reason to Tell the Truth?" 252.

2. See, e.g., Harland, *Superstructuralism*, 101–20, 155–66; Allan Megill, *Prophets of Extremity: Nietzsche, Heidegger, Foucault, Derrida* (Berkeley and Los Angeles: University of California Press, 1985), 181–256. For an altogether different story, one in which Foucault is neither a structuralist nor a poststructuralist, see Hubert L. Dreyfus and Paul Rabinow, *Michel Foucault: Beyond Structuralism and Hermeneutics* (2d ed.; Chicago: University of Chicago Press, 1983), esp. xi–xii, xxiv.

but comfortable in these vestments: "At the most, I am structuralism's 'altarboy,' " he protested.[3] Later, in the foreword to the English translation of his *Les Mots et les choses*, Foucault wryly laments the fact that "in France, certain half-witted 'commentators' persist in labelling me a 'structuralist.' "[4] And yet these half-wits had a point.

Throughout the 1960s, Foucault was struggling to articulate the largely unspoken and unwritten rules that determine the limits of what may be thought, said, or written in given historical periods—to articulate the conditions in which knowledge itself becomes possible, in other words, a system of conditions that he termed the *episteme* in *The Order of Things*, and the *archive* in *The Archaeology of Knowledge*.[5] This was at least a quasi-structuralist project, however, as Foucault himself conceded.[6] A recurrent preoccupation of French structuralism was the specification of the rules, codes, and conventions that underlie various sorts of meaning—the meaning of a folk tale, for example, or a marriage custom, or an item of dress—and make them possible.[7]

If Foucault was uncomfortable in the vestments of structuralism, he was in no hurry either to be ordained a "poststructuralist." He seems to have regarded the latter term as something of a signifier without a signified; "I do not understand what kind of problem is common to the people we call . . . post-structuralist," he once remarked.[8] Then, too, there was his Zen-like response when asked the question, "What is the origin of what we loosely call Post-Structuralism?" "Indeed, why not this term?" he replied, as we noted earlier.[9]

3. Quoted in Didier Eribon, *Michel Foucault*, trans. Betsy Wing (Cambridge, Mass.: Harvard University Press, 1991), 167.

4. Michel Foucault, *The Order of Things: An Archaeology of the Human Sciences*, trans. anon. (New York: Pantheon Books, 1970), xiv.

5. For more on these terms, see Foucault, *The Order of Things*, xxii, and *The Archaeology of Knowledge*, trans. Alan Sheridan (New York: Pantheon Books, 1972), 128–31.

6. Foucault admits in *The Archaeology of Knowledge* that his method "is not entirely foreign to what is called structural analysis" (15).

7. Foucault described his "archaeological" method as a search for the "underlying knowledge" that makes theories, practices, and institutions possible, "the stratum of knowledge that constitutes them historically" ("The Order of Things," in *Foucault Live*, 2).

8. Michel Foucault, "Critical Theory/Intellectual History," in *Politics, Philosophy, Culture: Interviews and Other Writings, 1977–1984*, ed. Lawrence D. Kritzman, trans. Alan Sheridan et al. (New York: Routledge, 1988), 34.

9. Foucault, "How Much Does It Cost for Reason to Tell the Truth?" 233.

This riposte neatly encapsulates Foucault's characteristic skepticism regarding "objects prior to discourse"—to use a phrase that recurs repeatedly in *The Archaeology of Knowledge*. In place of an "enigmatic treasure of 'things' anterior to discourse," the archaeologist of knowledge discovers "the regular formation of objects that emerge only in discourse."[10]

Indeed, Foucault's overriding concern throughout his career was to show how discourses of knowledge, which are also discourses of truth, covertly conspire to produce that which they purport to describe. In an interview conducted shortly before his death, he remarked:

> The political and social processes by which the Western European societies were put in order are not very apparent, have been forgotten, or have become habitual. They are a part of our most familiar landscape, and we don't perceive them anymore. . . . It is one of my targets to show people that a lot of things that are part of their landscape—that people think are universal—are the result of some very precise historical changes. All my analyses are against the idea of universal necessities in human existence. They show the arbitrariness of institutions and show which space of freedom we can still enjoy and how many changes can still be made.[11]

Foucault could never be accused of setting his sights too low. Prominent among the cultural landmarks and monuments that his work touched on, sometimes with a sledgehammer, more often with a chisel, were insanity, criminality, "man," authorship, sexuality, and even the body itself.[12]

10. Foucault, *The Archaeology of Knowledge*, 47.

11. Michel Foucault, "Truth, Power, Self: An Interview," in *Technologies of the Self: A Seminar with Michel Foucault*, ed. Luther H. Martin, Huck Gutman, and Patrick H. Hutton (Amherst: University of Massachusetts Press, 1988), 11.

12. On insanity, see Michel Foucault, *Madness and Civilization: A History of Insanity in the Age of Reason*, trans. Richard Howard (New York: Pantheon Books, 1965). On criminality, see *Discipline and Punish: The Birth of the Prison*, trans. Alan Sheridan (New York: Pantheon Books, 1977). On "man," see *The Order of Things* and cf. *The Archaeology of Knowledge*. On sexuality, see *The History of Sexuality*, trans. Robert Hurley (New York: Pantheon Books); vol. 1: *An Introduction*, 1978; vol. 2, *The Use of Pleasure*, 1985; and vol. 3, *The Care of the Self*, 1986. On the body, see *The Birth of the Clinic: An Archaeology of Medical Perception*, trans. Alan Sheridan (New

Take his history of insanity, for example. Foucault has no interest in affixing psychiatric labels to individuals or groups in earlier historical periods ("demoniacs," for instance), or in asking whether their disturbances "were identical with those known to us today."[13] Neither is he interested in "trying to reconstitute what madness itself might be."[14] To adopt either strategy would be to treat insanity as a stable referent that remains essentially the same from one historical period to the next. In Foucault's own baroque terms, it would be "to neutralize discourse, to make it the sign of something else, and to pierce through its density in order to reach what remains silently anterior to it."[15]

Instead, Foucault will attempt to relate insanity and other psychiatric phenomena "to the body of rules that enable them to form as objects of a discourse and thus constitute the conditions of their historical appearance."[16] What was necessary in order that the concept and phenomenon of insanity appear, ranting and raving, upon the stage of history? A complex congeries of forces, according to Foucault, certain "authorities of delimitation" in particular.[17] Prominent among these was modern medicine "as an institution possessing its own rules, as a group of individuals constituting the medical profession, as a body of knowledge and practice, as an authority recognized by public opinion, the law, and government."[18] Equally necessary were the modern legal codes, "penal law in particular," with its "definitions of excuse, non-responsibility, extenuating circumstances, and with the application of such notions as the *crime passionnel*, heredity, danger to society,"

York: Pantheon Books, 1973). Particularly pertinent for biblical scholarship, given its fascination with the figure of the author, is Foucault's excavation of the historical formation of the modern concept of authorship; see "What Is an Author?" in *Language, Counter-Memory, Practice: Selected Essays and Interviews*, ed. Donald F. Bouchard, trans. Donald F. Bouchard and Sherry Simon (Ithaca, N.Y.: Cornell University Press, 1977), 113–38. I have discussed the implications of this essay for biblical studies elsewhere; see Moore, *Literary Criticism and the Gospels*, 37–38, and *Mark and Luke in Poststructuralist Perspectives*, 146–49.

13. Foucault, *The Archaeology of Knowledge*, 47.
14. Ibid.
15. Ibid.
16. Ibid., 48.
17. Ibid., 41.
18. Ibid., 41–42.

and so on.[19] All of this had to be infused in turn with an enlightened eagerness to discriminate the pathological from the mystical, the corporeal from the spiritual, and the abnormal from the supernatural.[20]

Foucault's assaults on other, more solid-seeming "universals" (such as "man," sexuality, and the body) were conducted using a similar desolidifying solution of history mixed with skeptical philosophy. In general, whereas traditional histories of human thought have, to a greater or lesser extent, been histories of the more important things that human beings have discovered, Foucault's histories of human thought were histories of the more important things that human discourse has manufactured.

Foucault's project throughout was a Nietzschean one. "Nietzsche was a revelation to me," he admitted[21]—specifically the Nietzsche for whom every interpretation is but the interpretation of an interpretation. In an early sortie, "Nietzsche, Freud, Marx," Foucault hammers home the point: "There is nothing absolutely primary to be interpreted, since fundamentally everything is already interpretation," and so on.[22] In the period of Foucault's career that culminates in *The Archaeology of Knowledge*, he is principally concerned to show how modern discourses of knowledge have fabricated their objects of inquiry, as we have seen—thereby elaborating Nietzsche's claim that "There are no facts, only interpretations." In the second period of his career, which begins with the pivotal essay "Nietzsche, Genealogy, History,"[23] and continues through *Discipline and Punish* and the first volume of *The History of Sexuality*, Foucault shifts his attention to the manifold ways in which discourses of knowledge work through bodies to control entire populations—thereby elaborating Nietzsche's claim that every proclamation of a truth is the expression of a will to power.

---

19. Ibid., 42.

20. Ibid. For the complete story, see Foucault's *Madness and Civilization*.

21. Foucault, "Truth, Power, Self," 13.

22. Michel Foucault, "Nietzsche, Freud, Marx," in *Cahiers de Royaumont 6: Nietzsche* (Paris: Minuit, 1967), 189.

23. Michel Foucault, "Nietzsche, Genealogy, History," in *Language, Counter-Memory, Practice*, 139–64.

"POSTSTRUCTURALIST" FOUCAULT

To rephrase the foregoing shift in terms of the (un-Foucauldian) question posed earlier—where does structuralist Foucault end and poststructuralist Foucault begin?—one could say that after *The Archaeology of Knowledge*, although Foucault continues to be preoccupied with discourses of knowledge, these discourses no longer extend uninterruptedly to the horizon in every direction. Instead they are traversed by a force that is not simply reducible to discourse and is therefore all but inexpressible. Like Derrida and the later Lacan, Foucault now becomes obsessed with putting into language something that is properly irreducible to language—a recurrent poststructuralist concern, and one that brings poststructuralism into a peculiar relationship with theology.[24] For Foucault, this ineffable quantity is *power*, and its theater of operations is the body.

Foucault does not refer to either Saussure or Derrida as he reflects on power and its effects. For me, however, Foucault's formulation of power bears a striking resemblance both to Saussure's concept of language and to Derrida's concept of *différance*. For Saussure, as we have seen, language is a system of differences "without positive terms," which is to say that linguistic meaning is the product of linguistic differences; the elements of language have no meaning, no essence, in and of themselves. We have also seen how Derrida honed Saussure's theory of language, turning it into a scalpel with which to work on the flabby underbelly of Western metaphysics. Metaphysical concepts are pure effects of *différance*, for Derrida; they have no meaning, no essence, in and of themselves, and as such are neither primary nor fundamental.

Foucault's notion of power is no less differential or relational. What distinguishes Foucault from Saussure and Derrida, however, is that the differences and relations that preoccupy him are first and foremost social differences and relations—the inequalities and "disequilibriums" that characterize human interaction.[25] For Foucault, power is immanent in relationships—*all* relationships, however benign

---

24. For Derrida, this "something" is *différance*, as we have seen; for Lacan, it is the "Real." For a detailed account of the Real and its relationship to biblical theology, see The Bible and Culture Collective, *The Postmodern Bible* (New Haven, Conn.: Yale University Press, 1994).

25. Cf. Foucault, *The History of Sexuality*, 1:94.

they may seem: "[E]very human relation is to some degree a power relation."[26] Just how intimately are human beings bound up with the mechanisms and machinations of power? For Foucault, power is not something that is secondary or ancillary to individuals, an external force we deploy, or run up against, by turns. Rather, individuals are themselves effects of power; power as a relational force is what constitutes us:

> The individual is not to be conceived as a sort of elementary nucleus, a primitive atom, . . . on which power comes to fasten or against which it happens to strike. . . . In fact, it is already one of the prime effects of power that certain bodies, certain gestures, certain discourses, certain desires, come to be identified and constituted as individuals. The individual, that is, is not the *vis-à-vis* of power. . . . The individual is an effect of power.[27]

Here Foucault is remarkably close to Saussure, although he may not altogether realize it. For Saussure, the elementary particles of language are products of the differential relationships between them; similarly, for Foucault, individual subjects are products of a differential matrix of power relations—"differential" because it is characterized by "divisions, inequalities, and disequilibriums."[28]

Like Derrida and other poststructuralists, Foucault is determined to maintain the utter flatness of the differential plane that preoccupies him. This surface must have no privileged vantage points, no metaphysical peaks; "I never use the word power with a capital P," he explains.[29] Power must not be located on a mountaintop from whence it might issue directives engraved in stone: "Power's condition of possibility . . . must not be sought in the primary existence of a central point, in a unique source of sovereignty from which secondary and descendent forms would emanate."[30] Foucault's real target here is not the overt metaphysics of Judaism and Christianity, however ("you will

26. Michel Foucault, "Social Security," in *Politics, Philosophy, Culture*, 168.

27. Michel Foucault, "Two Lectures," in *Power/Knowledge*, 98.

28. Foucault, *The History of Sexuality*, 1:94. Needless to say, I am putting a certain spin on Foucault's description of power to bring out its Saussurean traits.

29. Michel Foucault, "The Question of Power," in *Foucault Live*, 185.

30. Foucault, *The History of Sexuality*, 1:93.

see the Son of Man seated at the right hand of the Power"—Mark 14:62), but the covert metaphysics of an altogether more formidable force in French intellectual life, namely Marxism, with its tendency to locate power in state apparatuses. Admonishing this unnamed audience, Foucault explains: "By power, I do not mean 'Power' as a group of institutions and mechanisms that ensure the subservience of the citizens of a given state," nor "a general system of domination exerted by one group over another."[31] These are but "the terminal forms power takes."[32] They are nodes in "the network of power relations . . . that passes through apparatuses and institutions, without being exactly localized in them."[33] Like the individual subject, therefore, the institutions of power, despite their apparent massiveness, are mere epiphenomenal effects for Foucault, spume on the surface of a shifting sea of "force relations"—one that is all surface, as it happens, with no heights or depths.

It would seem that Foucault wanted to formulate a theory of power utterly purged of metaphysical postulates. But this ascetic theory was purchased at considerable cost. Steven Best and Douglas Kellner echo the sentiments of many critics when they write:

> On Foucault's account, power is mostly treated as an impersonal and anonymous force which is exercised apart from the actions and intentions of human subjects. Foucault methodologically brackets the question of who controls and uses power for which interests to focus on the means by which it operates. Whatever new light this sheds in its emphasis that power operates in a diffuse force-field of relations of subjugation and struggle, it occludes the extent to which power is still controlled and administered by specific and identifiable agents in positions of economic and political power, such as members of corporate executive boards, bankers, the mass media, political lobbyists, land developers, or zealous outlaws in the Pentagon and White House.[34]

31. Ibid., 1:92.
32. Ibid.
33. Ibid., 1:96.
34. Steven Best and Douglas Kellner, *Postmodern Theory: Critical Interrogations* (New York: Guilford Press, 1991), 70. Similar criticisms of Foucault's theory of power have been advanced by feminist scholars; for a good example, see Nancy Hartsock, "Foucault on Power: A Theory for Women?" in *Feminism/Postmodernism*, ed. Linda J. Nicholson (New York: Routledge, 1990), 157–75.

Despite its counter-metaphysical thrust, moreover, Foucault's theory of power smacks strongly of secularized theology.[35] In the manner of a negative theologian, for example—a Pseudo-Dionysius or a Meister Eckhart—Foucault tells us what power is principally by telling us what it is not: "By power, I do not mean . . ."; "Power's conditions of possibility must not be sought in . . ."; "Power is not something that . . ."; and so on.[36] And his description of power is "positively" theological when he speaks of its ubiquity: "The omnipresence of power: not because it has the privilege of consolidating everything under its invincible unity, but because it is produced from one moment to the next, at every point, or rather in every relation from one point to another. Power is everywhere; not because it embraces everything, but because it comes from everywhere."[37] Derrida took elaborate "precautions" (his term) to avoid coming off sounding like a theologian, or a negative theologian, or even a negative atheologian. Foucault took few such precautions; small wonder, therefore, if his austere account of power bears a faint scent of incense.[38] But if Foucault's theory of power was excessively anemic and abstruse, his analyses of the workings of power in given historical periods were robust and concrete enough, as we shall see in the following chapter.

35. Cf. Jean Baudrillard, *Forget Foucault*, trans. Nicole Dufresne (New York: Semiotext[e], 1987), 59–60.
36. Foucault, *The History of Sexuality*, 1:92ff.
37. Ibid., 1:93.
38. Foucault himself twice compared his work to negative theology. What he had in mind, however, was not his conception of power, but his critique of the humanist conception of "man." Foucault saw humanism as a displaced theology, the "birth of man" coinciding with the "death of God." In *The Order of Things*, especially, Foucault is out to subvert humanism's faith in this divinized "man," just as negative theologians once sought to subvert comfortable traditional conceptions of God. Foucault first invoked this analogy in "La Pensée du dehors," *Critique* 229 (1966): 526–27, and reintroduced it in an unpublished lecture given at the Collège de France in 1980. For a detailed exegesis of the analogy, see James Bernauer, "The Prisons of Man: An Introduction to Michel Foucault's Negative Theology," *International Philosophical Quarterly* (December 1987): 365–80; and idem, "Michel Foucault's Ecstatic Thinking," in *The Final Foucault*, ed. James Bernauer and David Rasmussen (Cambridge, Mass.: MIT Press, 1987), 67ff. The latter discussion reappears, slightly modified, in Bernauer's *Michel Foucault's Force of Flight: Toward an Ethics for Thought* (Atlantic Highlands, N.J.: Humanities Press International, 1990), 178ff.

In the final period of his career, Foucault's interests shifted once again, this time from "technologies of power, which determine the conduct of individuals and submit them to certain ends or domination," to "technologies of the self, which permit individuals to effect by their own means or with the help of others a certain number of operations on their own bodies and souls, thoughts, conduct, and way of being, so as to transform themselves in order to attain a certain state of happiness, purity, wisdom, perfection, or immortality."[39] In consequence, Foucault began to turn his attention to "technologies of the self" in Greek and Roman antiquity and in Christianity, late medieval and early modern Christianity in particular, but also early Christianity—although he steered clear of the New Testament, preferring to confine himself to patristic and early monastic writings. A fourth volume of his *History of Sexuality*, devoted to Christianity and entitled *Les Aveux de la chair* (The confessions of the flesh), remained unfinished at his death in 1984.

Frequently, I find Foucault's statements on Christianity—those that have found their way into print—to be disappointingly bland, a litany of often uncontroversial assertions that lack the edge characteristic of his best work.[40] Foucault does make at least one fascinating claim regarding Christianity, but I will hold it over for the end of the following chapter. In that chapter I shall be attempting to read a central New Testament theme—the power of the cross—through the lens not of Foucault's explicit statements on Christianity, for the most part, but of his sharpest and strongest book, which is largely silent on Christianity. That book is *Discipline and Punish*,[41] and its natural dialogue partner is Paul, as we shall see. Indeed, rather than introduce Foucault to Paul, I hope to show that they are already deep in conversation.

39. Michel Foucault, "Technologies of the Self," in *Technologies of the Self*, 18.

40. For a dollop of this bland fare, see Foucault, "Technologies of the Self," 40. Foucault's other statements on Christianity, usually more provocative, include ibid., 39–49; "Politics and Reason," in *Politics, Philosophy, Culture*, 60–73; and "The Subject and Power," in Dreyfus and Rabinow, *Michel Foucault*, 213–15. Other comments can be found scattered throughout the three volumes of *History of Sexuality*. Still others occur in hard-to-obtain sources. Bernauer notes and quotes many of these sources in "Michel Foucault's Ecstatic Thinking" (reprinted and retouched in Bernauer, *Michel Foucault's Force of Flight*, 158–84).

41. Foucault referred to it as his "foremost book" (see "The Concern for Truth," in *Foucault Live*, 303).

5

POSTSTRUCTURALIST HISTORIOGRAPHY: FOUCAULT _{THE}^{AT} FOOT _{THE}^{OF} CROSS

MY FATHER was a butcher. As a child, the inner geographical boundaries of my world extended from the massive granite bulk of the Redemptorist church squatting at one end of our street to the butcher shop guarding the other end. Redemption, expiation, sacrifice, slaughter . . . There was no city abattoir in Limerick in those days; each butcher did his own slaughtering. I recall the hooks, the knives, the cleavers; the terror in the eyes of the victim; my own fear that I was afraid to show; the crude stun gun slick with grease; the stunned victim collapsing to its knees; the slitting of the throat; the filling of the basins with blood; the skinning and evisceration of the corpse; the wooden barrels overflowing with entrails; the crimson floor littered with hooves.

I also recall a Good Friday sermon by a Redemptorist preacher that recounted at remarkable length the atrocious agony felt by our sensitive Savior as the nails were driven through his hands and feet. Strange to say, it was this recital, and not the other spectacle, that finally caused me to faint. Helped outside by my father, I vomited gratefully on the steps of the church.

"THE UTTERLY VILE DEATH OF THE CROSS"

The central symbol of Christianity is the figure of a tortured man. Attending an exhibition of instruments of torture in Rome, Page duBois reports: "I gazed uneasily at the others visiting this spot. . . . I tried to imagine what brought them there. Was it a historical curiosity about the Middle Ages, or the same desire that brings people to horror movies, or sexual desire invested in bondage and discipline? I was there too."[1] Such unease would be almost unimaginable in a Sunday service, and yet the central spectacle is not altogether dissimilar. The Gospels may have contributed to the profound equanimity with which the average Christian views this grisly spectacle; "they crucified him" is the extraordinarily restrained testimony of the evangelists (Mark 15:24; Matt. 27:35; Luke 23:33; John 19:18). Martin Hengel has written what amounts to a book-length elaboration of this stark statement.[2]

The burden of Hengel's *Crucifixion* is to show, through extensive appeal to ancient sources, why crucifixion was regarded as the most horrific form of punishment in the ancient world.[3] Far from being a dispassionate execution of justice, "crucifixion satisfied the primitive lust for revenge and the sadistic cruelty of individual rulers and of the masses."[4]

> Even in the Roman empire, where there might be said to be some kind of "norm" for the course of the execution (it included a flogging beforehand, and the victim often carried the beam to the place of execution, where he was nailed to it with outstretched arms, raised up and seated on a small wooden peg), the form of execution could vary considerably: crucifixion was a punishment in which the caprice and sadism of the executioners were given full rein. All attempts to give a perfect description of *the* crucifixion in archaeological terms

1. Page duBois, *Torture and Truth* (New York: Routledge, 1991), 2.

2. Martin Hengel, *Crucifixion in the Ancient World and the Folly of the Message of the Cross*, trans. John Bowden (Philadelphia: Fortress Press, 1977). When I tracked down this book in the college library I was surprised to find that it was not shelved in the religion section, as I had expected, but in a corner of the history section devoted to torture. Hengel's theological monograph was flanked by illustrated treatises on medieval torture, on the one hand, and Amnesty International reports, on the other.

3. The German edition of the work bore the Latin title *Mors turpissima crucis*, "the utterly vile death of the cross," a quotation from Origen (*Commentary on St. Matthew* 27.22). Josephus similarly deemed crucifixion "the most wretched of deaths" (*The Jewish War* 7.203), while Cicero called it "that most cruel and disgusting penalty," and "the ultimate punishment" (*In Verrem* 2.5.165, 168).

4. Hengel, *Crucifixion in the Ancient World*, 87.

are therefore in vain; there were too many different possibilities for the executioner.[5]

The implication, of course, is that the bald statement "they crucified [Jesus]" may still retain some of its secrets even when the historians and archaeologists are through interrogating it. In a chapter unambiguously titled "Crucifixion as a 'Barbaric' Form of Execution of Utmost Cruelty," Hengel documents some of the possibilities open to the executioner.[6]

SPECTACLE AND SURVEILLANCE

... the crowds who had gathered there for the spectacle ...

—Luke 23:48

Seventeen hundred years later we find the executioners exploring other possibilities. Foucault's *Discipline and Punish* opens with the following scene:

> On 2 March 1757 Damiens the regicide was condemned "to make the *amende honorable* before the main door of the Church of Paris," where he was to be "taken and conveyed in a cart, wearing nothing but a shirt, holding a torch of burning wax weighing two pounds"; then, "in the said cart, to the Place de Grève, where, on a scaffold that will be erected there, the flesh will be torn from his breasts, arms, thighs and calves with red-hot pincers, his right hand, holding the knife with which he committed the said parricide, burnt with sulphur, and, on those places where the flesh will be torn away, poured molten lead, boiling oil, burning resin, wax and sulphur melted together and then his body drawn and quartered by four horses and his limbs and body consumed by fire, reduced to ashes and his ashes thrown to the winds."[7]

According to witnesses, the execution was badly botched; the quartering went on interminably, two more horses had to be brought in, "and when that did not suffice, they were forced, in order to cut off the wretch's thighs, to sever the sinews and hack at the joints."[8] The victim, meanwhile, forgave his executioners, Jesus-like, and begged them not to swear as they struggled to dismember him.

5. Ibid., 25.
6. Ibid., 22–32.
7. Foucault, *Discipline and Punish*, 3.
8. Ibid.

In time, as Foucault reports, the ritual of public torture became intolerable. "Protests against the public executions proliferated in the second half of the eighteenth century: among the philosophers and theoreticians of the law; among lawyers and *parlementaires*; in popular petitions and among the legislators of the assemblies."[9] The more spectacular forms of public execution gradually ceased, and judicial punishment was reestablished on a more "humane" foundation. "In the worst of murderers, there is one thing, at least, to be respected when one punishes: his 'humanity.' The day was to come, in the nineteenth century, when this 'man,' discovered in the criminal, would become the target of penal intervention, the object that it claimed to correct and transform, the domain of a whole series of 'criminological' sciences."[10] No longer could judicial punishment be justified as the rightful vengeance of a sovereign on a rebellious subject.

A giant step forward in the history of judicial practice? Foucault does not think so, which is what makes *Discipline and Punish* remarkable. For Foucault, the feudal "society of the spectacle" was succeeded in the modern period by something altogether more sinister. The fearful spectacle of brutal punishment being publicly exacted on the body of a condemned criminal had at least the advantage of being open and direct. The degree of covert control over the individual that modern "disciplinary societies" aspire to would have been unimaginable under the old regimes. In particular, for Foucault, the prison reforms of the nineteenth century concealed an iron fist of totalitarianism in a velvet glove of humanitarianism. "In the totally ordered, hierocratized space of the nineteenth-century prison, the prisoner is put under constant surveillance, discipline, and education in order to transform him into what power as now organized in society demands that everyone become: docile, productive, hard-working, self-regulating, conscience-ridden, in a word, 'normal' in every way."[11]

In a 1978 interview, Foucault remarked: "I'm delighted that historians found no major error in [*Discipline and Punish*] and that, at the same time, prisoners read it in their cells."[12] Recently, however,

9. Ibid., 73.
10. Ibid., 74.
11. Hayden White, "Michel Foucault," in *Structuralism and Since*, 106.
12. Michel Foucault, "On Power," in *Politics, Philosophy, Culture*, 101.

Page duBois has questioned the story that *Discipline and Punish* tells. She notes that the tripartite structure of the book shows "Torture" (the subject matter of Part One) yielding first to "Punishment" (Part Two) and then to "Discipline" (Part Three), the implication being that state-sanctioned atrocities such as the execution by torture of transgressors have now receded into history, "that we are all so thoroughly disciplined now, have so deeply internalized our own policing, that we no longer need the spectacle of punishment."[13] Foucault states confidently: "We are now far away from the country of tortures, dotted with wheels, gibbets, gallows, pillories."[14] "Tell it to the El Salvadorans," replies duBois.[15] In other words, the narrative of *Discipline and Punish* "is resolutely Eurocentric"; Foucault's "description of the transition from spectacular torture and execution to internalized discipline remains a local analysis."[16]

His narrative is further undermined by the fact that whereas state-sanctioned torture does indeed seem to be the exception rather than the rule today in Western Europe and North America, the substantial role that certain Western democracies have played in supporting regimes that routinely employ torture to enforce public order suggests a disturbing, symbiotic relationship between the "societies of the spectacle" and the "disciplinary societies," one that the seductive chronology of *Discipline and Punish* obscures.[17]

These are serious criticisms. At the very least, they caution us that if we are to use *Discipline and Punish* as an analogical tool for a reconsideration of the relationship between violent punishment and internalized self-policing in the New Testament (I shall be confining myself to the letters of Paul), we must allow for the possibility that the relationship may be symbiotic or parasitic.

13. DuBois, *Torture and Truth*, 153.
14. Foucault, *Discipline and Punish*, 307.
15. DuBois, *Torture and Truth*, 154.
16. Ibid. Foucault himself was not unaware of this: "I could perfectly well call my subject [in *Discipline and Punish*] the history of penal policy in France—alone" ("Questions on Geography," in *Power/Knowledge*, 67).
17. Cf. DuBois, *Torture and Truth*, 154–57.

"HIS MIGHTY AND ANNIHILATING REACTION"

Let us begin with Hengel's conclusion, which is that "the earliest Christian message of the crucified messiah demonstrated the 'solidarity' of the love of God with the unspeakable suffering of those who were tortured and put to death by human cruelty."[18] This is a moving interpretation of the crucifixion. It is complicated by a troubling question, however, one that Hengel can ill afford to raise, having already argued that crucifixion "is a manifestation of trans-subjective evil, a form of execution which manifests the demonic character of human cruelty and bestiality."[19] The question is a simple one: Who inflicted the punishment of crucifixion on Jesus? Was it the procurator of Judea, acting on behalf of the Roman emperor? Or was it an even higher power, acting through the Roman authorities (cf. John 19:11; Acts 4:27-28; Rom. 13:1; 1 Cor. 2:8)?[20]

To interpret Jesus' death as punishment is to move within the ambit of the doctrine of atonement. Although it had a rich patristic history,[21] the doctrine came fully into its own only with Saint Anselm's *Cur Deus Homo?* (1097–98), where it was formulated as a "theory of satisfaction." The Anselmian form of the doctrine has generally been accepted by Roman Catholic theologians since the Middle Ages.[22] Moreover, as Gustaf Aulén notes, it has long been argued "that a continuous line may be traced from Anselm, through medieval scholasticism, and through the Reformation, to the Protestant 'Orthodoxy' of the seventeenth century."[23] This is not to say, continues Aulén, that

18. Hengel, *Crucifixion in the Ancient World*, 88.
19. Ibid., 87.
20. Whether "the rulers of this age" in 1 Cor. 2:8 are to be understood as human authorities, supernatural authorities (cf. Col. 2:15), or a combination of both does not substantially affect the issue.
21. See Francis M. Young, *The Use of Sacrificial Ideas in Greek Christian Writers from the New Testament to John Chrysostom* (Cambridge, Mass.: Philadelphia Patristic Foundation, 1979).
22. It has been adopted by the Roman Catholic magisterium although "not actually defined" (Karl Rahner and Herbert Vorgrimler, *Dictionary of Theology*, trans. Richard Strachan et al. [2d ed.; New York: Crossroad, 1981], 463).
23. Gustaf Aulén, *Christus Victor: An Historical Study of the Three Main Types of the Idea of the Atonement*, trans. A. G. Herbert (New York: Macmillan, 1940), 18.

Anselm's teaching was merely regurgitated by his successors, "for differences of view are noted in Thomas Aquinas and in the Nominalists, and the post-Reformation statements of the doctrine have a character of their own; nevertheless, there is a continuity of tradition, and the basis of it is that which Anselm laid."[24] What Anselm laid can be paraphrased as follows:

> Sin is an offence against the majesty of God. In spite of his goodness, God cannot pardon sin without compounding with honor and justice. On the other hand, he cannot revenge himself on man for his offended honor; for sin is an offence of infinite degree, and therefore demands infinite satisfaction; which means that he must either destroy humanity or inflict upon it the eternal punishments of hell. . . . There is but one way for God to escape this dilemma without affecting his honor, and that is to arrange for some kind of *satisfaction*. He must have infinite satisfaction because the offence is immeasurable. . . . Hence, the necessity of the *incarnation*. God becomes man in Christ; Christ suffers and dies in our stead.[25]

It is, of course, no coincidence that Anselm's interpretation of the crucifixion bears a marked resemblance to the feudal conception of judicial punishment as outlined in the opening chapters of *Discipline and Punish*. Under the feudal regime, "the law . . . represented the will of the sovereign; he who violated it must answer to the wrath of the king. . . . Thus, the power and integrity of the law were reasserted; the affront was righted. This excessive power found its form in the ritual of atrocity."[26] The term "ritual" is highly appropriate here. "Under this type of regime the notion of crime is still not fully distinguished from that of sacrilege, so that punishment takes the form of a ritual intended not to 'reform' the offender but to express and restore the sanctity of the law which has been broken."[27]

---

24. Ibid., 18–19. Salient statements of the Reformers on the atonement are reproduced in Pierre Grelot, *Péché originel et rédemption examinés à partir de l'Epître aux Romains: Essais Théologiques* (Paris: Declée, 1973), 205ff.

25. From the Introduction to Saint Anselm, *Proslogium; Monologium; an Appendix on Behalf of the Fool by Gaunilon; and Cur Deus Homo?* trans. Sidney Norton Deane and James Gardiner Vose (La Salle, Ill.: Open Court, 1951), viii.

26. Dreyfus and Rabinow, *Michel Foucault*, 145.

27. Sarup, *Post-Structuralism and Postmodernism*, 74, paraphrasing Foucault. Foucault himself uses language such as the following: "[T]orture forms part of a ritual. It is an element in the liturgy of punishment" (*Discipline and Punish*, 34).

The language of wrath and punishment applied to the crucifixion is by no means extinct even among critical exegetes. In his massive commentary on Romans, Douglas Moo has recently defended the traditional attribution to Paul of a doctrine of divine wrath and retribution, while attacking the revisionist school of thought that would reject or qualify this attribution.[28] Moo quotes approvingly Anders Nygren's paraphrase of Romans 1:18: "As long as God is God, He cannot behold with indifference that His creation is destroyed and His holy will trodden underfoot. Therefore He meets sin with his mighty and annihilating reaction."[29] Here we are not far from the world of Anselm, whatever about the world of Paul. We can almost hear the bones cracking on the wheel as the might of the offended sovereign bears down upon the body of the condemned.

"WHAT A PRIMITIVE MYTHOLOGY"

Not surprisingly, the doctrine of atonement has been an acute embarrassment for many other twentieth-century exegetes. Rudolf Bultmann is exemplary in this regard.[30] Traditionally the doctrine has been laid squarely at the feet of Paul. For Bultmann, as for the majority of critical

28. Douglas Moo, *Romans 1–8* (Chicago: Moody Press, 1991), 94. He singles out C. H. Dodd (*The Epistle of Paul to the Romans* [London: Hodder & Stoughton, 1932]) as representative of this influential school of thought. A more current example would be James D. G. Dunn, for whom Paul's conception of God's wrath is a highly nuanced affair, transcending the commonplace notions of "divine indignation" and "judicial anger against evil," not to mention divine vengeance (*Romans 1–8* [Dallas: Word Books, 1988]), 54-55, 70-71).

29. Anders Nygren, *Commentary on Romans* (Philadelphia: Fortress Press, 1949), 98.

30. So too Xavier Léon-Dufour, whose *Life and Death in the New Testament* (trans. Terrence Prendergast; San Francisco: Harper & Row, 1986) I shall briefly discuss later in this section. This embarrassment is less pronounced in other New Testament studies that deal with the atonement, such as Vincent Taylor, *The Atonement in New Testament Teaching* (London: Epworth, 1940), Martin Hengel, *The Atonement: The Origins of the Doctrine in the New Testament*, trans. John Bowden (Philadelphia: Fortress Press, 1981), and Kenneth Grayston, *Dying, We Live: A New Enquiry into the Death of Christ in the New Testament* (Oxford: Oxford University Press, 1990).

scholars, Paul does not altogether deserve this dubious honor.[31] Paul's thought regarding sin contains two distinct strands, according to Bultmann, and these strands "are not harmonized with each other."[32] Most significant for us is the strand that Bultmann regards as least important; he concedes that there is in Paul a "juristic conception of death as the punishment for sin."[33] This Paul inherited from the "Old Testament-Jewish tradition."[34] Bultmann continues:

> *Death is the punishment for the sin a man has committed*; sinners are "worthy of death" (Rom. 1:32 KJ), they have "earned" death. So Paul can also say that . . . the sinner by his death pays his debt, atones for his sin (Rom. 6:7). In such statements, death, we must recognize, is first thought of as the death which is natural dying, as Rom. 5:12ff. shows, according to which death as the punishment for sin was brought into the world by Adam's sin. Nevertheless, they also presuppose that this death will be confirmed—made final, so to say—by the verdict condemning them to "destruction" which God will pronounce over sinners on the judgment day (Rom. 2:6-11).[35]

Faced with this grim prospect, the sinner is in urgent need of justification through the blood of Jesus Christ, "a propitiatory sacrifice by which forgiveness of sins is brought about; which is to say: by which the guilt contracted by sins is canceled."[36] Closely bound up with the idea of propitiatory sacrifice, moreover, is the idea of vicarious sacrifice, "which likewise has its origin in the field of cultic-juristic thinking."[37] "The same phrase (*hyper hēmōn*) that is translated 'for us' can also express this idea, meaning now: 'instead of us,' 'in place of us.'"[38] Bultmann detects a vicarious theology in Gal. 3:13 ("becoming a curse in our stead") and 2 Cor. 5:21 ("he made him who

31. The following discussion is indebted to Robert H. Gundry's critique of Bultmann in his *Soma in Biblical Theology: With Emphasis on Pauline Anthropology* (New York: Cambridge University Press, 1976); see esp. 206–9.

32. Rudolf Bultmann, *Theology of the New Testament*, trans. Kendrick Grobel (New York: Charles Scribner's Sons, 1951), 1:249.

33. Ibid.

34. Ibid., 1:246.

35. Ibid., his emphasis.

36. Ibid., 1:295. According to Bultmann, this view underlies the following Pauline passages: Rom. 3:25ff., 5:9; 1 Cor. 11:24ff., 15:3; 2 Cor. 5:14; cf. Rom. 4:25, 5:6, 8; 8:32; 14:15; Gal. 1:4; 2:20; 1 Thess. 5:10.

37. Ibid., 1:296.

38. Ibid.

was unacquainted with sin to be sin in our stead"; cf. Rom. 8:3), and argues that both ideas, vicarious and propitiatory sacrifice, merge in 2 Cor. 5:14ff.[39]

Bultmann himself has little time for such ideas. "How can the guilt of one man be expiated by the death of another who is sinless—if indeed one may speak of a sinless man at all?" he asks in some exasperation in "New Testament and Mythology." "What primitive notions of guilt and righteousness does this imply? And what primitive idea of God? . . . What a primitive mythology it is, that a divine Being should . . . atone for the sins of men through his own blood!"[40] The sacrificial hypothesis entails a *sacrificium intellectus* that Bultmann is determined to avoid.

In his *Theology of the New Testament*, therefore, Bultmann is careful to highlight those passages in which Paul appears to interpret Jesus' crucifixion as potential deliverance from the *power of sin*, and to gloss over passages in which Paul appears to interpret the crucifixion as sacrificial atonement for *actual sins committed*. The latter passages do "not contain Paul's characteristic view."[41] For Paul, "Christ's death is not merely a sacrifice which cancels the guilt of sin (i.e., the punishment contracted by sinning), but is also *the means of release from the powers of this age: Law, Sin, and Death*."[42] Like the judicial reformers of the eighteenth century, then, Bultmann finds the idea of a vengeful sovereign, one capable of inflicting brutal physical punishment on his rebellious subjects, to be intolerable. Such primitive ideas "make the Christian faith unintelligible and unacceptable to the modern world."[43]

"Once you suppress the idea of vengeance," writes Madan Sarup, "punishment can only have a meaning within a technology of reform"[44]—or a *theology* of reform, as here. The doctrine of atonement, in its classic medieval form, amounts to an interpretation of Jesus'

39. Ibid.

40. Rudolf Bultmann, "New Testament and Mythology," in *Kerygma and Myth: A Theological Debate*, ed. Hans Werner Bartsch, trans. Reginald H. Fuller (New York: Harper & Row, 1961), 7.

41. Bultmann, *Theology of the New Testament*, 1:296.

42. Ibid., 1:297–98, his emphasis.

43. Bultmann, "New Testament and Mythology," 5.

44. Sarup, *Post-Structuralism and Postmodernism*, 74, paraphrasing Foucault.

death as public execution by torture for transgression, the righting of an affront to the sovereign power—the injured party not being the Roman emperor, however (as those who administer the punishment unwittingly suppose), but the Divine Majesty Himself. Uncomfortable with such primitive notions, Bultmann prefers to attribute to Paul— the "real" Paul—an interpretation of Jesus' death as a potential reform, a unique opportunity for the transgressor to be utterly transformed from within. The event of the cross promises freedom from sin. "But this freedom is not a static quality: it is freedom *to obey*. The indicative implies an imperative."[45] A horrific act of violence, then, execution by public torture, gives birth to an altogether different order in which obedient action springs spontaneously from within and no longer from any external coercion. This is also the transition that *Discipline and Punish* describes.

Bultmann's insistence that the crucifixion be understood in terms of inner transformation recalls the "subjective" doctrine of the atonement, commonly associated with the twelfth-century philosopher and theologian Peter Abelard, and distinguished from Anselm's "objective" doctrine. Abelard interpreted the atonement "as consisting essentially in a change taking place in men rather than a changed attitude on the part of God."[46] The subjective doctrine only came into its own during the Enlightenment, however, when, as we have seen, the practice of public execution by torture was being questioned: "A 'more human' idea of the Atonement was propounded. . . . The doctrine of retributive punishment was scouted, for punishment could only be ameliorative."[47] Around the same time, moreover, an aspect of the traditional doctrine of hell, one defended by such eminent theologians as Augustine, Aquinas, and Peter of Lombardy, became an embarrassment in certain quarters. This was the idea "that part of the happiness of the blessed consists in contemplating the torments of the damned" (cf. Rev. 14:9-10; Luke 16:23-26; Isa. 66:24), a spectacle calculated to fill them with grim satisfaction, or outright pleasure,

45. Bultmann, "New Testament and Mythology," 32, his emphasis. This sentiment is, of course, a commonplace of Pauline studies.
46. Aulén, *Christus Victor*, 18.
47. Ibid., 150.

since it manifests the Divine Sovereign's impartial justice and implacable hatred of sin.[48]

Howard Eilberg-Schwartz, introducing *The Savage in Judaism*, remarks: "[T]he work of deconstructive critics . . . and Foucault . . . has taught me that the key to a tradition often lies in what it excludes."[49] Can it be that the key to the Pauline interpretation of Jesus' crucifixion, as reconstructed by biblical scholars such as Bultmann, lies in what that reconstruction excludes or plays down, namely, the "Jewish sacrificial" element in Paul's thought?[50] At least since the Enlightenment, Christian theology and philosophy have tended to regard certain aspects of ancient Jewish religion as "savage" (whether or not that word is used), as Eilberg-Schwartz has shown.[51] The practice of sacrifice in particular has caused Christian apologists much discomfort: "On the one hand, this practice certainly appears barbaric and crude and has parallels in the practices of savages. On the other hand, the Christian revelation [as commonly interpreted] is itself premised on the idea that God sacrificed a son as expiation for the world."[52] What precisely is it about this premise that tends to make critical exegetes uncomfortable? Bultmann has already directed us to the answer. A glance at Xavier Léon-Dufour's *Life and Death in the New Testament* will help us to see it more clearly.

Léon-Dufour's monograph returns repeatedly to the motifs of sacrifice, expiation, and atonement. For Bultmann, the sacrifical elements in Paul's theology were unpalatable remnants of the "Old Testament-Jewish tradition." Léon-Dufour is still more squeamish about

48. D. P. Walker, *The Decline of Hell: Seventeenth-Century Discussions of Eternal Torment* (Chicago: University of Chicago Press, 1964), 29.

49. Howard Eilberg-Schwartz, *The Savage in Judaism: An Anthropology of Israelite Religion and Ancient Judaism* (Bloomington and Indianapolis: Indiana University Press, 1990), 25.

50. In Bultmann's case, this exclusion is especially troubling. Is it possible to isolate Bultmann's statements on Paul in "New Testament and Mythology" (later elaborated in his *Theology of the New Testament*) from the Nazi solution to the Jewish question, which was being implemented even as Bultmann wrote? What is Bultmann really doing in these statements? Excising an undesirable Jewish influence from Paul's thought? Furthering the civilizing ethnic cleansing everywhere under way around him? These are difficult questions that I would like to return to on another occasion.

51. Eilberg-Schwartz, *The Savage in Judaism*, 31–86.

52. Ibid., 55.

the blood of Jesus. "We must carefully refrain from regarding this 'blood' from the perspective of the bloody sacrifices in other religions, or even within the framework of Jewish sacrifices," he cautions.[53] "To give expression to Christ's death there is no need now to refer to the sacrifices of the Old Testament, except to note their end, their disappearance."[54] Léon-Dufour is pained by a common tendency among Christians, loosely based on a sacrificial reading of Paul,[55] to speak "of sin's 'offense' against God and of God's intention to punish and to chastise," on the one hand, and "of 'reparation,' of 'satisfaction,' and of 'merit' by which the human Jesus 'satisfied' divine justice," on the other hand.[56] This leads to a "distressing attribution" to God of "inadmissible dispositions."[57]

Although Léon-Dufour does not say so explicitly, the dispositions in question are those of a cruel despot who keeps his fearful subjects in check through the threat of frightful physical punishment— the sort of despot who features prominently in the early chapters of *Discipline and Punish*. Interestingly, the public executions by torture in eighteenth-century France led to the precise phenomenon that Léon-Dufour deplores, an attribution to the sovereign of "inadmissible dispositions." Foucault writes: "It was as if the punishment was thought to equal, if not to exceed, in savagery the crime itself, to accustom the spectators to a ferocity from which one wished to divert them, . . . to make the executioner resemble a criminal, judges murderers."[58] Léon-Dufour's God is not given to theatrical displays of power. A "healthy understanding of Jesus' death" would emphasize instead its transformative potential, how it is "active" in the believer through baptism and the Eucharist "so that it exercises its influence in ordinary life."[59] Once again, as in the eighteenth-century rhetoric of judicial reform,

53. Léon-Dufour, *Life and Death in the New Testament*, 189.
54. Ibid., 190.
55. A "Paul" who is also the author of Hebrews.
56. Léon-Dufour, *Life and Death in the New Testament*, 192.
57. Ibid.
58. Foucault, *Discipline and Punish*, 9.
59. Léon-Dufour, *Life and Death in the New Testament*, 192. Compare Dunn on Rom. 6:4: "We should note at once how quickly Paul jumps from a deep theological concept (union with Christ in his death) to talk of daily conduct. For Paul, evidently, *the character of daily conduct is actually determined by these deeper realities*" (*Romans 1–8*, 330, his emphasis).

the recommended shift of emphasis is from corporal punishment ("painful to a more or less horrible degree," as one contemporary glossed it)[60] to internal reform leading to a transformation of everyday behavior.

"The key to a tradition often lies in what it excludes." What is it that the transformational interpretation of the crucifixion excludes? Is it the issue of power, an issue all too close to the surface in the punitive interpretation, the power of one person over the body of another, a power never more evident than in the relationship of the torturer to the victim—and never more disturbing, perhaps, than when the torturer is God and the victim God's Son? But what if the transformation of the believer were merely a more efficient exercise of power, still exercised on the body but now reaching into the psyche as well to fashion acceptable thoughts and attitudes yielding acceptable behavior, of power absolutized to a degree unimaginable even in a situation of extreme physical torture? This, above all, is the question that *Discipline and Punish* prompts us to ask.

DISCIPLINE AND DISCIPLESHIP

> Are they ministers of Christ? . . . I am a better one: with far greater labors, far more imprisonments, with countless floggings, and often near death. Five times I have received from the Jews the forty lashes minus one. Three times I was beaten with rods.
>
> —*2 Cor. 11:23-25*

Let us rephrase the question: What if the crucified Jesus, as interpreted by Paul, were actually God's own (pri)son? The prison would contain a courtyard, and the courtyard would be dominated by a scaffold. Needless to say, Paul's gospel of reform cannot simply be equated with the judicial reforms of the eighteenth century. For the latter, the punitive liturgy of public torture had to be consigned once and for all to history. But for Paul, discipline remains indissolubly bound up with atrocity. Each believer must be subjected to public execution by torture: "Do you not know that all of us who have been baptized into Christ Jesus were baptized into his death?" (Rom. 6:3). Paul refuses to separate torture from reform (cf. 1 Cor. 1:18ff.; Gal. 2:19-21). Unless the

60. Quoted in Foucault, *Discipline and Punish*, 33.

believer is tortured to death in the (pri)son, he or she cannot be rehabilitated: "We know that our old self was crucified with him so that the sinful body might be destroyed [*hina katargēthē to sōma tēs hamartias*]" (Rom. 6:6; cf. Gal. 5:24).

Of course, Christian discipline is also bound up with power: "[T]he kingdom of God does not consist in talk but in power [*en dynamei*]" (1 Cor. 4:20, RSV). How is this power exercised and who is entitled to exercise it? Foucault's views on power may be pertinent here. "In thinking of the mechanisms of power," he explains, "I am thinking . . . of its capillary forms of existence, the point where power reaches into the very grain of individuals, touches their bodies."[61] For Foucault, "nothing is more material, physical, corporal than the exercise of power"[62]—and for Paul, too, seemingly. As Elizabeth A. Castelli has remarked of 1 Corinthians, "the human body provides a central series of images and themes for this text. . . . Food practices and sexuality occupy fully half of the letter's content. . . . It is also the case that explicit language about authority and power is used most frequently in the discussion of bodily practices."[63]

Discipline has only one purpose, according to Foucault: the production of "docile bodies."[64] "A body is docile that may be subjected, used, transformed and improved," says Foucault.[65] "I punish my body and enslave [*doulagōgō*] it," says Paul (1 Cor. 9:27). Indeed, the docility engendered by discipline is precisely that of the slave.[66] "[W]hoever was free when called is a slave [*doulos*] of Christ," says Paul (1 Cor. 7:22), he himself being no exception (Rom. 1:1; cf. Phil. 1:1). Of course, there are slaves and "slaves" (cf. 1 Cor. 7:21-24; Philem. 15-16), and Paul is in the parenthesized category. Even among "slaves," moreover, a strict hierarchy is observed; the man is the "head" [*kephalē*] of the woman, for example, even as Christ is the "head" of the man (1 Cor. 11:3; 14:34). Christ himself is also a subject: "When all things are subjected to him, then the Son himself will also be subjected to the one who put all things in subjection under him" (1 Cor. 15:28; cf. 11:3).

61. Michel Foucault, "Prison Talk," in *Power/Knowledge*, 39.
62. Michel Foucault, "Body/Power," in *Power/Knowledge*, 57–58.
63. Castelli, "Interpretations of Power in 1 Corinthians," 209.
64. Cf. Foucault, *Discipline and Punish*, 135–69.
65. Ibid., 136.
66. Just as crucifixion in the Roman world was, above all, "the slaves' punishment" (Cicero, *In Verrem* 2.5.169). Through Jesus' crucifixion, the Christian slave is disciplined and kept in line.

Even when Jesus' crucifixion is interpreted as a means toward internalized discipline, then, rather than as retributive punishment for sin (and Paul is not uncomfortable with the latter interpretation), absolute power continues to be attributed to a monarchical God. The question that inevitably arises is, Who stands to benefit from this attribution? To appeal to one's own exemplary subjection to a conveniently absent authority in order to legitimate the subjection of others is a strategy as ancient as it is suspect. "Be imitators [*mimētai*] of me, as I am of Christ," says Paul (1 Cor. 11:1; cf. 1 Cor. 4:16; 1 Thess. 1:6). Above all, imitate my obedience by obeying me (cf. 1 Cor. 11:16; 14:37-38).[67]

"It has often been said that Christianity brought into being a code of ethics fundamentally different from that of the ancient world," writes Foucault, adding that what is less often noted is that Christianity "spread new power relations throughout the ancient world."[68] This new form of power Foucault terms pastoral power. It "is not merely a form of power which commands; it must also be prepared to sacrifice itself for the life and salvation of the flock. Therefore, it is different from royal power, which demands a sacrifice from its subjects to save the throne."[69] Ultimately, for Foucault, "this form of power cannot be exercised without knowing the inside of people's minds, without exploring their souls, without making them reveal their innermost secrets. It implies a knowledge of the conscience and an ability to direct it."[70] Foucault is thinking particularly of the sacrament of penance here,[71] which assumed the status of a Christian obligation only after the Fourth Lateran Council in 1215 C.E., but which is deeply rooted in the ancient Jewish conception of an all-seeing God who searches and tests the human heart, exposing its innermost secrets (cf. 1 Sam. 16:7; 1 Kings 8:39; 1 Chron. 28:9; Pss. 17:3, 26:2, 44:21, 139:1-2,23; Prov. 15:11; Jer. 11:20, 12:3, 17:10).

67. Castelli builds a Foucauldian reading of Paul on this motif; see *Imitating Paul: A Discourse of Power* (Louisville: Westminster/John Knox Press, 1991).
68. Foucault, "The Subject and Power," 214.
69. Ibid.
70. Ibid. For more on pastoral power, see Foucault, "Politics and Reason," 60ff.
71. This is clear from Foucault, "Technologies of the Self," 40–41.

Although this tradition does not achieve anything like its full flowering in Paul—that will have to await the institution of private confession—Paul does allude to it frequently (e.g., Rom. 2:16, 29, 8:27; 1 Cor. 4:5, 14:25). In time, Paul's ecclesiastical descendents will appropriate for themselves the divine privilege of laying bare the human soul. "Since the Middle Ages at least, Western societies have established the confession as one of the main rituals we rely on for the production of truth."[72] But this form of discipline too will be closely bound up with atrocity: "One confesses—or is forced to confess. When it is not spontaneous or dictated by some internal imperative, the confession is wrung from a person by violence or threat; it is driven from its hiding place in the soul, or extracted from the body. Since the Middle Ages, torture has accompanied it like a shadow, and supported it when it could go no further: the dark twins."[73]

Eventually, Foucault argues, this coercive obsession with the state of the soul becomes the soul of the modern state. His hypothesis is that "the modern Western state has integrated in a new political shape, an old power technique," namely, pastoral power, with its investment in the regulation of the individual's inner existence.[74] This power technique, "which over centuries—for more than a millennium—had been linked to a defined religious institution, suddenly spread out into the whole social body; it found support in a multitude of institutions."[75]

As it happens, these are the same institutions of surveillance and control that Foucault has repeatedly attacked in his writings. Of course, they are not necessarily the institutions that ordinarily leap to mind in this connection—the KGB, the CIA, and so forth. As we have seen, power is at its most insidious and efficient, for Foucault, precisely

72. Foucault, *The History of Sexuality*, 1:58.
73. Ibid., 1:59.
74. Foucault, "The Subject and Power," 213. The symbol of the modern state, for Foucault, or better, of the "disciplinary society," is the Panopticon, Jeremy Bentham's utopian design for the perfect disciplinary institution. In the Panopticon, the inmates would be totally and permanently visible to supervisors who themselves would normally be invisible (*Discipline and Punish*, 195–228). On the connections between the Panopticon and the all-seeing God of Judaism and Christianity, see Moore, *Mark and Luke in Poststructuralist Perspectives*, 129–44.
75. Foucault, "The Subject and Power," 215.

when its workings are effaced—when its brow is furrowed with humanitarian concern, when its voice is warm with Christian compassion, when its menace is masked even, or especially, from itself. The institutions at which Foucault has taken aim in his writings, therefore, are particularly those in which power wears a white coat and a professional smile. They include psychiatry, the secular sacrament of penance, and the target of his first major work, *Madness and Civilization*; modern medicine, which exposes the innermost secrets of the human body to the scientific gaze, and the subject of his next book, *The Birth of the Clinic*; the social sciences, which likewise turn the human subject into an object of scientific scrutiny, and the target of his third major work, *The Order of Things*; modern methods of dealing with delinquency and criminality, the subject of *Discipline and Punish*; and the modern policing of sexual "normality,"the subject of the first volume of his *History of Sexuality*.

Foucault once confessed in an interview: "A nightmare has pursued me since childhood: I have under my eyes a text that I can't read, or of which only a tiny part can be deciphered; I pretend to read it, but I know that I'm inventing."[76] Foucault tempts us to invent in our turn, to write preludes and sequels to his own surreal historical narrative, one in which the melancholy murmur of a medieval penitential liturgy is heard echoing through the contemporary halls of science, of medicine, and of justice—the public dismemberment of the body of the deviant having been displaced by strategies of social control that seem to grow ever lighter the deeper they extend into each of us.[77]

EPILOGUE

I recall that each ornate confessional in the Redemptorist church displayed, deep in its somber interior, the effigy of a tortured man, and that the column of confessionals was itself flanked by the fourteen Stations of the Cross, each one ornate and imposing, the spectacle of atrocity being inseparable, as I now realize, from the spectacle of docility, "the quiet game of the well behaved."[78]

76. Michel Foucault, "The Discourse of History," in *Foucault Live*, 25.

77. Their touch is lightest of all in the case of television, a "disciplinary technology" that Foucault never examined. The obverse of Paul's panoptic God, television's single blind eye polices and controls, not by being all-seeing, but by being seen by all.

78. Foucault, *Discipline and Punish*, 69.

CONCLUSION:
CRITICISM TERMINABLE
AND INTERMINABLE

[I]s there such a thing as a natural end to an analysis—is there any
possibility at all of bringing an analysis to such an end?

—*Sigmund Freud*[1]

AS CRITICS of the New Testament, just how critical should
we be? Where should we draw the line? At the point at which central
tenets of traditional Christian faith begin to crack under the unaccus-
tomed strain—faith that Jesus did indeed rise from the dead, for example? In 1906 Albert Schweitzer published his iconoclastic classic,
Von Reimarus zu Wrede, better known to Anglophone readers as *The
Quest of the Historical Jesus*.[2] Twenty-five years later, we find an aging
Schweitzer ruminating sadly, but stoically, on the "unrest and difficulty
for Christian piety" occasioned by his skeptical *Quest*:

> Truth is under all circumstances more valuable than nontruth, and
> this must apply to truth in the realm of history as to other kinds of
> truth. Even if it comes in a guise which piety finds strange and at

1. Sigmund Freud, "Analysis Terminable and Interminable," in *Standard Edition*, 23:219.
2. Albert Schweitzer, *Von Reimarus zu Wrede* (Tübingen: J. C. B.
Mohr, 1906); trans. W. Montgomery as *The Quest of the Historical Jesus: A
Critical Study of Its Progress from Reimarus to Wrede* (London: A. & C. Black,
1910).

first makes difficulties for her, the final result can never mean injury; it can only mean greater depth. Religion has, therefore, no reason for trying to avoid coming to terms with historical truth.[3]

While I no longer share Schweitzer's sanguine certainty that Christianity has nothing to fear from "historical truth," I do empathize with his intense preoccupation with the truth-claims of Christianity. This fascination first led me to historical criticism, and afterwards led me to poststructuralism.

Few events in my life have been more liberating than the discovery of historical criticism. My first exposure to critical biblical scholarship occurred while I was a novice monk in a Cistercian monastery high in the Knockmealdown mountains of southeast Ireland. At the time I was convinced that it was God's will that I remain forever in the monastery. Indeed, I tended to identify His will with the (very) solid masonry of the building: to step outside the monastery gates, never to return, would be to step outside God's will and to be separated from Him for all eternity. Furthermore, since I had been deeply involved in the Catholic Charismatic Renewal prior to entering the monastery, and heavily involved with drugs, especially hallucinogens, before that again, God was constantly speaking to me. To open my Bible at random was to be assured of yet another "word from the Lord." I was deeply happy and thoroughly miserable.

In time, I stumbled upon some stray crumbs of biblical scholarship in the bowels of the monastery library—Bernhard Anderson's *Understanding the Old Testament* and Dennis Nineham's commentary on Mark—and adopted them as *lectio divina*. Translated, this means that it took me almost six months to pray my way through Anderson and another four to make it through Nineham. Daily I could feel the stays of my soul expanding to accommodate this startling new knowledge, and eventually some of the snaps began to burst. The day I finally left the monastery was one of great exhilaration and deep sadness, and I've been running and stumbling ever since.

Historical criticism of the Bible has often been said to be an inch wide and a mile deep. Personally, I cannot claim to have descended the full mile. After several years of inching through the pipe, I felt it

---

3. Albert Schweitzer, *Out of My Life and Thought: An Autobiography*, trans. C. T. Campion (New York: Holt, Rinehart and Winston, 1961), 45.

was becoming narrower and narrower, and I anxiously began to look for an outlet.

The "new literary criticism" of the New Testament—narrative criticism, for the most part, coupled with reader-response criticism— seemed, for a time, to be that outlet. Soon, however, a sneaking suspicion began to creep up on me in the darkness of that second tunnel: What if narrative criticism were actually a retreat from the critical rigor of historical scholarship? What if its not inconsiderable success were due to a widespread weariness with "the unrest and difficulty for Christian piety" caused by centuries of historical criticism? With the appearance in 1990 of Mark Allan Powell's *What Is Narrative Criticism?* I found unexpected confirmation of my suspicion.

In the final chapter of his book, Powell grapples with an interesting question: "What effect will the use of this method [narrative criticism] have on the wider task of interpreting Scripture for the life of the church?"[4] A highly salubrious effect, according to Powell. Narrative criticism, on his account, turns out to be surprisingly compatible with "the interests of believing communities."[5] It "is especially attractive to those who have been uncomfortable with the challenges posed by historical criticism."[6]

Particularly striking, for me, is the confessional twist that Powell manages to give to two of narrative criticism's salient traits. First he has this to say of narrative criticism's trademark preoccupation with the "final form" of the biblical text: "By focusing on the finished form of the text, narrative criticism seeks to interpret Scripture at its canonical level; the text that is considered is identical with that which believing communities identify as authoritative for their faith and practice."[7] Powell also gives a theological twist to the preoccupation with the role of the reader that is characteristic both of narrative criticism and reader-response criticism. He notes "the certainty of faith with which the Gospel narratives appear to have been written and with which they obviously expect to be read."[8] And he adds: "By interpreting texts from the point of view of their own implied readers, narrative

4. Powell, *What Is Narrative Criticism?* 85.
5. Ibid., 88.
6. Ibid.
7. Ibid.; cf. 85–86.
8. Ibid., 88.

criticism offers exegesis that is inevitably from a faith perspective."[9] At this point, poststructuralism begins to back away nervously from narrative criticism, alarmed at the evangelical glint that has abruptly appeared in its eye.[10]

To reiterate what I said in the Introduction, the new literary criticism of the New Testament, particularly in its reader-oriented forms, represents a remarkably smooth extension of redaction criticism—smoother than most redaction critics realize. For it amounts to an explicit assumption of the redaction critic's implicit task of reenacting the role of reading implied, encoded, or inscribed in a biblical text, of becoming the ideal or intended audience of that text—of submitting to the rule of the text and the authority of its author (or Author?). But what if the text in question were ethically flawed? What if it were misogynistic, say, or anti-Jewish?[11] Is it not also necessary to read against the ideological grain of the biblical text at times, to set aside the traditional task of reconstructing the author's intention— of reverently reenacting the role of reading rhetorically inscribed in the text? As I tried to show in chapter 2—my attempt to swim against the current of the living water discourse in the Fourth Gospel—deconstruction is uniquely well equipped for such counter-reading, or "resisting reading," as the feminist critic Judith Fetterly has dubbed it.[12]

9. Ibid., 88–89. Too late, he runs to shut the stable door: "We should be careful, however, not to disparage historical criticism simply because it raises questions that are difficult for people of faith. The struggles that historical-critical investigation engender are significant for theological growth. Employment of narrative criticism as a means of avoiding difficult or controversial issues represents, in my mind, a misuse of the methodology" (89).

10. Granted, Powell is not claiming to speak for all narrative critics. He does find support for his position in certain statements by Alan Culpepper, however (*What Is Narrative Criticism?* 88, 90–91), and he could have drawn on other prominent narrative critics as well, notably, Jack Dean Kingsbury and Robert Tannehill (see Moore, *Literary Criticism and the Gospels*, 58–59).

11. Powell would argue that narrative criticism can "salvage" the alleged anti-Jewish passages in Matthew, for example, along with other scriptural passages "that would otherwise be difficult for members of believing communities to accept," by "interpreting them in terms of their intended literary effect rather than their apparent historical reference" (*What Is Narrative Criticism?* 88; cf. 66–67). Fred W. Burnett, who also brings narrative criticism to bear on the Matthean problem, arrives at a very different conclusion, however; see "Exposing the Anti-Jewish Ideology of Matthew's Implied Author: The Characterization of God as Father," *Semeia* 59 (1992): 155–91.

12. Judith Fetterly, *The Resisting Reader: A Feminist Approach to American Fiction* (Bloomington: Indiana University Press, 1978).

The feature of poststructuralism that draws me most strongly, however, is essentially the same feature that once drew me to historical criticism. I refer to the latter's shape-shifting ability to make the familiar seem startlingly strange, books of the Holy Bible suddenly acquiring human (all too human) authors, ghostwriters, copy editors, places and dates of publication—everything, in short, but an ISBN number. But poststructuralism's powers of redescription exceed even those of historical criticism. As David Clines has recently pointed out, while historical criticism did succeed in defamiliarizing the Bible to an impressive extent "by locating it in a cultural context alien to our own, it did not ever defamiliarize most of its theological ideas (witness the persistence in current theological discourse of ideas of retribution, covenant, sin, the maleness of God, metaphors of the king and warrior for the divine)."[13] Poststructuralism, however, is able to push this project of defamiliarization fully into the realm of theology, as I attempted to show both in chapter 1, my account of Derrida's exposure of the extent to which theology and metaphysics infect all our attempts to think critically, and in chapter 5, my Foucauldian redescription of "the power of the cross" as it has been construed by Paul and certain of his ecclesiastical and critical successors.

What, then, is the precise relationship of poststructuralism to historical criticism? As I see it, poststructuralism is temperamentally unsuited to be yet another handmaid (a French maid?) to historical criticism. Neither is poststructuralism poised to become historical criticism's slayer (historical criticism is much too massive for that, occupying entire city blocks at the national conferences; it crushes its enemies by sitting on them). Rather, in the context of biblical studies, poststructuralism would be historical criticism's id, the seat of its strongest antiauthoritarian instincts—historical criticism unfettered at last from the ecclesiastical superego that has always compelled it to genuflect before the icons it had come to destroy.

13. David J. A. Clines, "Possibilities and Priorities of Biblical Interpretation in an International Perspective," *Biblical Interpretation* 1 (1993): 85. Neither, for that matter, did historical criticism ever defamiliarize most of its seminal methodological assumptions: witness the persistence, even in current biblical studies, of such problematic notions as the possibility of scholarly neutrality and objectivity, the recoverability of "hard" historical facts, the recoverability of authorial intentions, and so on.

FURTHER READING: POSTDECONSTRUCTURALISM AND BEYOND

Beyond the straits of poststructuralism, it is rumored, is a poorly mapped region called postmodernism. Some take this sea for a pond, as we shall discover. But first some further soundings in the swollen literature on poststructuralism.

MORE DERRIDA AND FOUCAULT

Personally, I have found Jonathan Culler's *On Deconstruction: Theory and Criticism after Structuralism* (Ithaca, N.Y.: Cornell University Press, 1982) to be the most serviceable of the standard introductions to deconstruction. Culler's opening critique of reader-response criticism from a deconstructionist angle is essential reading for anyone wishing to do sophisticated, reader-oriented work on the Bible, as is Elizabeth Freund's *The Return of the Reader: Reader-Response Criticism* (New York: Methuen, 1987), also written from a deconstructionist perspective. The best advanced introduction to deconstruction is *Jacques Derrida* by Geoffrey Bennington and Derrida himself (Chicago: University of Chicago Press, 1992). Bennington does the introducing and Derrida provides an oblique running commentary on Bennington's efforts.

Random diving into Derrida's own oeuvre can result in painful bellyflops, as I know from experience. A relatively easy place to slip in is Peggy Kamuf's *A Derrida Reader: Between the Blinds* (New York: Columbia University Press, 1990), twenty-two essays and book excerpts from Derrida, each with an editorial lead-in. "Plato's Pharmacy" in *Dissemination* (Chicago: University of Chicago Press, 1981) is vintage Derrida, and a highly suggestive example for biblical criticism. Derrida has written on, or around, the Bible himself; three of these sorties in particular are worth mentioning. First, "Edmond Jabès and the Question of the Book" in *Writing and Difference* (Chicago: University of Chicago Press, 1978), a personal favorite of mine; the imagery is frequently extraordinary. Second, "Des Tours de Babel" (*Semeia* 54 [1991]), probably the most accessible of Derrida's biblical forays (it's in English, despite the title). Finally, "Of an Apocalyptic Tone Recently Adopted in Philosophy," which appeared in an earlier issue of *Semeia* (23 [1982]) on *Derrida and Biblical Studies*, tackles Kant and the book of Revelation in tandem.

Excellent on the connections and disconnections between deconstruction, on the one hand, and feminist and liberationist exegesis, on the other, is David Jobling's "Writing the Wrongs of the World: The Deconstruction of the Biblical Text in the Context of Liberation Theologies" (*Semeia* 51 [1990]). Susan Lochrie Graham also fuses feminist and deconstructionist strategies in her "Silent Voices: Women in the Gospel of Mark" (*Semeia* 54 [1991]). Various other deconstructive readings of biblical texts are listed in my *Literary Criticism and the Gospels: The Theoretical Challenge* (New Haven, Conn.: Yale University Press, 1989) and *Mark and Luke in Poststructuralist Perspectives: Jesus Begins to Write* (New Haven, Conn.: Yale University Press, 1992). Still others are listed in the 940-page *Jacques Derrida: An Annotated Primary and Secondary Bibliography*, compiled by William Schultz and Lewis L. B. Fried (Hamden, Conn.: Garland Publishing, 1992).

Well before *A Derrida Reader*, there was *The Foucault Reader*, edited by Paul Rabinow (New York: Pantheon Books, 1984). It includes Foucault's "What Is an Author?" a sobering read for any biblical scholar. Another good place to dip into Foucault is "The Subject and Power," a concise statement of his aims with some interesting asides on Christianity. It appears as an Afterword to Hubert L. Dreyfus and Paul Rabinow's *Michel Foucault: Beyond Structuralism and Hermeneutics* (2d ed.; Chicago: University of Chicago Press, 1983).

Advanced introductions to Foucault abound. I especially like Allan Megill's treatment of Foucault in *Prophets of Extremity: Nietzsche, Heidegger, Foucault, Derrida* (Berkeley and Los Angeles: University of California Press, 1985), and Steven Best and Douglas

Kellner's rough handling of him in *Postmodern Theory: Critical Interrogations* (New York: Guilford Press, 1991). Of the many books devoted exclusively to Foucault, three stand out from the pack: Dreyfus and Rabinow's *Michel Foucault* for its indefatigable detail; Gilles Deleuze's *Foucault* (Minneapolis: University of Minnesota Press, 1988) for its sophistication; and James W. Bernauer's *Michel Foucault's Force of Flight: Toward an Ethics for Thought* (Atlantic Highlands, N.J.: Humanities Press International, 1990) for its (rare) coverage of Foucault's work on Christianity.

Two other books provide useful critical perspectives on Foucault: *Feminism and Foucault: Reflections on Resistance*, edited by Irene Diamond and Lee Quinby (Boston: Northeastern University Press, 1988), and *After Foucault: Humanistic Knowledge, Postmodern Challenges*, edited by Jonathan Arac (New Brunswick, N.J.: Rutgers University Press, 1988). Two biographies of Foucault have also appeared: Didier Eribon's *Michel Foucault* (Cambridge, Mass.: Harvard University Press, 1991) and James Miller's *The Passion of Michel Foucault* (New York: Simon & Schuster, 1992). The latter is the more lurid of the two, dwelling at length on Foucault's homosexuality and his fascination with sadomasochism; surprisingly, it is also the more theoretically astute.

Elizabeth A. Castelli has produced two Foucauldian studies of Paul: *Imitating Paul: A Discourse of Power* (Louisville: Westminster/John Knox Press, 1991) and "Interpretations of Power in 1 Corinthians." The latter appears in *Semeia* 54 (1991), which is devoted to *Poststructuralism as Exegesis* and features two further articles that borrow from Foucault, one by Regina Schwartz, the other by me. Foucault also crops up frequently in *Semeia* 57 and 58 (1992), a double issue on *Discursive Formations, Ascetic Piety and the Interpretation of Early Christian Literature*; see especially the contributions of Carol A. Newsom and Geoffrey Galt Harpham. Also worth reading is David J. Leigh's "Michel Foucault and the Study of Literature and Theology," which appeared in *Christianity & Literature* 33 (1983).

OTHER POSTSTRUCTURALISTS

To date, more than fifty books have appeared on Jacques Lacan in English alone. By now I've read more Lacan than I can ever "use" in my work—a poor investment, no doubt, but intellectually very rewarding.

The best introductory essay on Lacan that I know of is Malcolm Bowie's "Jacques Lacan" in *Structuralism and Since: From Lévi-Strauss to Derrida*, edited by John Sturrock (New York: Oxford University Press, 1979). Especially suggestive for biblical exegesis is James M. Mellard's *Using Lacan, Reading Fiction* (Urbana and Chicago: University of Illinois Press, 1991). Elizabeth Grosz's *Jacques Lacan: A Feminist Introduction* (New York: Routledge, 1990) is useful for other reasons.

The most exhaustive account of Lacanian theory is Ellie Ragland-Sullivan's *Jacques Lacan and the Philosophy of Psychoanalysis* (Urbana and Chicago: University of Illinois Press, 1986), and the most exhaustive account of Lacan, the man, is Elisabeth Roudinesco's *Jacques Lacan & Co.: A History of Psychoanalysis in France, 1925–1985* (Chicago: University of Chicago Press, 1990). The smartest book on Lacan is Jane Gallop's *The Daughter's Seduction: Feminism and Psychoanalysis* (Ithaca, N.Y.: Cornell University Press, 1982), but the most personal and personable is Gallop's *Reading Lacan* (Ithaca, N.Y.: Cornell University Press, 1985). The liveliest book on Lacan is Catherine Clément's *The Lives and Legends of Jacques Lacan* (New York: Columbia University Press, 1983), but the most colorful is Slavoj Žižek's *Enjoy Your Symptom! Jacques Lacan in Hollywood and Out* (New York: Routledge, 1992).

Good places to dip into Lacan himself include "The Agency of the Letter in the Unconscious or Reason Since Freud" in *Écrits: A Selection* (New York: Norton, 1977), or "The Seminar on 'The Purloined Letter,' " now in *The Purloined Poe: Lacan, Derrida, and Psychoanalytic Reading*, edited by John P. Muller and William J. Richardson (Baltimore: Johns Hopkins University Press, 1988). Like Derrida, Lacan's style is frequently impenetrable, but, on a good day, remarkably lyrical. He has pronounced on the Bible more than once; try his interpretation of the binding of Isaac, for example, in his "Introduction to the Names-of-the-Father Seminar," now in *Television/A Challenge to the Psychoanalytic Establishment* (New York: Norton, 1990). A detailed discussion of Lacan and the Bible is forthcoming in The Bible and Culture Collective's *The Postmodern Bible* (New Haven, Conn.: Yale University Press, 1994). Lacan also features prominently in my *Mark and Luke in Poststructuralist Perspectives*, while close encounters between Lacan and philosophical theology occur in *Lacan and Theological Discourse*, edited by Edith Wyschogrod, David Crownfield, and Carl A. Raschke (Albany: SUNY Press, 1989), and in Mark C. Taylor's *Altarity* (Chicago: University of Chicago Press, 1987).

Roland Barthes and Julia Kristeva have also written on the Bible. Barthes's two biblical essays, "Wrestling with the Angel: Textual Analysis of Genesis 32:23-33" and "The Structural Analysis of Narrative: Apropos of Acts 10-11," show him straddling the hairline chasm between structuralism and poststructuralism; both essays can be found in his *The Semiotic Challenge* (New York: Hill and Wang, 1988). The best book on Barthes that I've come across is Michael Moriarty's *Roland Barthes* (Stanford, Calif.: Stanford University Press, 1991). Kristeva has written more extensively on the Bible; her most important biblical work can be found in *Tales of Love* (New York: Columbia University Press, 1987), and especially in *Powers of Horror: An Essay on Abjection* (New York: Columbia University Press, 1982).

Kristeva is frequently associated with two other French feminists, Hélène Cixous and Luce Irigaray. Their work has had an enormous impact on feminist debate in North American academic circles. Irigaray has also written on the Bible and theology. Her biblical work, along with Kristeva's, is surveyed in *The Postmodern Bible*. Two other recent books are also worth consulting: *Transfigurations: Theology and the French Feminists*, edited by C. W. Maggie Kim, Susan St. Ville, and Susan Simonaitis (Minneapolis: Fortress Press, 1993), and *Body/Text in Julia Kristeva: Religion, Women, and Psychoanalysis*, edited by David Crownfield (Albany: SUNY Press, 1992).

Earlier in her career, Kristeva was associated with a radical theory of intertextuality; see her collection, *Séméiotiké: Recherches pour une sémanalyse* (Paris: Seuil, 1969), two essays of which are translated in *Desire in Language: A Semiotic Approach to Literature and Art* (New York: Columbia University Press, 1980). Intertextuality is not what it used to be; the term now trips off the tongues even of conservative biblical scholars discussing the Synoptic problem. Less domesticated breeds of intertextuality can be glimpsed in *Influence and Intertextuality in Literary History*, edited by Jay Clayton and Eric Rothstein (Madison: University of Wisconsin Press, 1991). The book opens with a valuable survey and critique of different theories of intertextuality, including those of Kristeva, Barthes, Derrida, and Foucault, contrasting them with the older idea of "influence." It might be read alongside *Intertextuality in Biblical Writings: Essays in Honor of Bas van Iersel*, edited by Sipke Draisma (Kampen, the Netherlands: Kok Pharos, 1989), or *Reading between Texts: Intertextuality and the Hebrew Bible*, edited by Danna Nolan Fewell (Louisville: Westminster/ John Knox Press, 1992).

The New Historicism, a relatively recent, high-profile development in American literary studies, can be regarded as yet another variant of poststructuralism. Introductions include H. Aram Veeser's opening salvo in *The New Historicism* (New York: Routledge, 1989), which Veeser also edits; Louis Montrose's subtly nuanced "New Historicisms" in *Redrawing the Boundaries: The Transformation of English and American Literary Studies*, edited by Stephen Greenblatt and Giles Gunn (New York: MLA Publications, 1992); and Brook Thomas's critical *The New Historicism and Other Old-Fashioned Topics* (Princeton, N.J.: Princeton University Press, 1991). *A New Historicism Reader* is also forthcoming from Routledge, again edited by Veeser. A prestigious New Historicist journal, *Representations*, and a monograph series, "The New Historicism: Studies in Cultural Poetics," are both published by the University of California Press. Mary Ann Tolbert has attempted to harness New Historicist insights for a reading of Mark's Gethsemane episode in "The Gospel in Greco-Roman Culture," in *The Book and the Text: The Bible and Literary Theory*, edited by Regina Schwartz (Cambridge, Mass.: Basil Blackwell, 1990).

Still other poststructuralists can be found huddled in "More Post-Structuralists," the final chapter of Richard Harland's *Superstructuralism: The Philosophy of Structuralism and Post-Structuralism* (New York: Methuen, 1987). These include Gilles Deleuze and Félix Guattari, whose remarkable book, *A Thousand Plateaus: Capitalism and Schizophrenia* (Minneapolis: University of Minnesota Press, 1987), touches on the Bible and the biblical tradition at several points; and Jean Baudrillard, whose work, Harland tells us with a stutter, may be regarded as "Post-Post-Structuralist."

POSTMODERNISM

In 1986 I came to America once again, eager this time to stay. When the time came to present myself at the Temple, I set out for the Joint

Annual Meeting of the American Academy of Religion and the Society of Biblical Literature, which was being held that year in Atlanta. It was my first experience of that colossal cerebral carnival. I arrived in time to hear Gary Phillips unwrap his presentation, "Deconstruction and the Parables of Jesus," for a dubious Literary Aspects of the Gospels and Acts Group. I already knew something about deconstruction, enough to say some silly things about it in my dissertation. What impressed me most about Phillips's paper, however, was its preamble, an attempt to situate poststructuralism in relation to the debate on postmodernism then gathering momentum in the humanities. Listening to Phillips that day, I decided that poststructuralism was, after all, but a single sharp horn on a lesser head of the beast from the sea—although now I would tend to see it more as a small Francophile franchise in a gigantic global shopping mall. In any case, the postmodernism debate remains, for me, the ultimate wide-angle lens through which to view what it is we do as biblical critics.

But what *is* postmodernism? For a potpourri of answers and a quick tour of the terrain, try one, or all, of the following: *Postmodernism: A Reader*, edited by Thomas Docherty (New York: Columbia University Press, 1993); *A Postmodern Reader,* edited by Joseph Natoli and Linda Hutcheon (Albany: SUNY Press, 1993); and *Postmodernism: A Reader,* edited by Patricia Waugh (New York: Edward Arnold, 1992). Pauline Marie Rosenau's *Post-Modernism and the Social Sciences: Insights, Inroads, and Intrusions* (Princeton, N.J.: Princeton University Press, 1992) also covers a great deal of ground in a relatively short span of text.

Of the avalanche of books that have appeared on postmodernism, two have been written by biblical scholars. James Breech's *Jesus and Postmodernism* (Minneapolis: Fortress Press, 1989) is an all-out attack on the beast, hardly surprising given Breech's (skewed) conception of what it is: a conviction that "death is God." For Edgar V. McKnight in his *Postmodern Use of the Bible: The Emergence of Reader-Oriented Criticism* (Nashville: Abingdon Press, 1988), the essence of postmodernism is a radical reader-oriented literary criticism. Fred W. Burnett is closer to the mark, it seems to me, when he suggests in his "Postmodern Biblical Exegesis: The Eve of Historical Criticism" that reader-response criticism is the last "decompression chamber" for many biblical critics before they surface into postmodernism (*Semeia*

51 (1990]). The postmodernism Burnett has in mind is epitomized by poststructuralism, and this is also how Phillips sees it in his "Exegesis as Critical Praxis: Reclaiming History and Text from a Postmodern Perspective" (*Semeia* 51 [1990]).

The equation of poststructuralism with quintessential postmodernism seems to work best when we limit our conception of modernism to the values, assumptions, and ideals inherited from the Scientific Revolution and the Enlightenment, the progenitors of our own discipline of biblical studies. The most penetrating account of this brand of modernism would be Timothy Reiss's *The Discourse of Modernism* (Ithaca, N.Y.: Cornell University Press, 1982), and the most celebrated account of what has succeeded it would be Jean-François Lyotard's *The Postmodern Condition: A Report on Knowledge* (Minneapolis: University of Minnesota Press, 1984), with its definition of postmodernism as "incredulity toward metanarratives," especially those of the Enlightenment. The poststructuralist exemplar of this brand of postmodernism would, I suppose, be Foucault, who worked directly and extensively on the Enlightenment legacy (see David Couzens Hoy's "Foucault: Modern or Postmodern?" in *After Foucault*).

More often than not, however, the term *modernism*, as used in the postmodernism debate, denotes an aesthetic phenomenon—literary art roughly since Flaubert, visual art roughly since Manet, and their deconstruction of verbal and visual language, respectively. How is poststructuralism related to this form of modernism? It would seem to be inextricably intertwined with it. French poststructuralism can be interpreted as a displaced reenactment of the modernist revolution in the arts, which was exhausted and at an impasse by the 1960s. For example, when Roland Barthes comes to stage "The Death of the Author" in 1968 (the essay is now in his *Image—Music—Text* [New York: Noonday Press, 1977]), he enlists as his accomplices Mallarmé, Proust, the Surrealists, and other modernist writers and artists. In similar ways, Derrida, Kristeva, and other poststructuralists have translated modernist aesthetics into critical discourse, as I argue in my article, "The 'Post-'Age Stamp: Does It Stick? Biblical Studies and the Postmodernism Debate" (*Journal of the American Academy of Religion* 57 [1989]). The most incisive account of this translation project, however, occurs in Andreas Huyssen's "Mapping the Postmodern," which appears both in his *After the Great Divide: Modernism, Mass Culture,*

Postmodernism (Bloomington: Indiana University Press, 1986) and in
Natoli and Hutcheon's *A Postmodern Reader.*

Inseparable from postmodernism's epistemological and aesthetic trajectories are its political trajectories. Robert M.
Fowler cites
as a "grand index" of the postmodern in biblical studies the fact that
many have begun to awake from the Enlightenment dream of disin-
terested inquiry and objective truth, roused especially by "First World"
feminist and minority scholars, but increasingly, too, by a still-muted
chorus of Latin American, African, and Asian voices ("Postmodern
Biblical Criticism," *Forum* 5 [1989]). This claim is elaborated in much
greater detail by The Bible and Culture Collective in their *Postmodern
Bible.*

In the voluminous literature on postmodernism, however, popular culture has loomed far larger than feminism or any other form of
political criticism. To get a real feel for pop postmodernism, one must
turn to the popular and alternative press—to the *Utne Reader's* cover
section, "Postmodernism and Beyond" (July/August 1989), for example, which chronicles the "Late Postmodern Era" in terms of landmarks such as the following: "*November 1986*: November issue of
Elle combines the adjective *postmodern* with the words *ski* and *parka*,
indicating the meaninglessness of the former and the desirability of
the latter." In short, not all the energy coursing through the gigantic
body of postmodernism is positive, something with which most biblical
postmodernists have yet to come to terms. For many outside our field,
postmodernism is first and foremost a global cultural phenomenon,
one whose signal features include mass media, mass culture, infor-
mation technology, and multinational capitalism. This electronic and
economic hydra is the protagonist of Fredric Jameson's epic, *Postmodernism, or, The Cultural Logic of Late Capitalism* (Durham, N.C.:
Duke University Press, 1991), the most ambitious and most adequate
account of postmodernism to date, and a challenge to those of us in
biblical studies who use the term to add flesh and muscle to our often
emaciated conceptions of what it means.

GLOSSARY

Archaeology: Michel Foucault's early term, borrowed from Kant, for his project—that of excavating some of the more solid-seeming features of our cultural landscape (such as "man," the body, insanity) in order to reveal their constructed nature.

Deconstruction: Jacques Derrida's term for his philosophical project, an ambitious attempt to disturb some of the most familiar habits of thought in Western culture, notably, our reliance on hierarchical oppositions (presence/absence, primary/secondary, central/marginal, etc.). In the 1970s and early 1980s, large numbers of North American literary critics began to "deconstruct" literary texts, taking their lead mainly from Derrida's readings of certain philosophical texts. (Derrida's own relationship to literature is more complex; finding the literature that most interests him to be more advanced philosophically than most philosophy, he prefers to mine it rather than deconstruct it.) Deconstruction is especially interested in the exclusions, omissions, and blind spots that enable texts—and societies—to function. American deconstruction also modeled itself on the writings of Paul de Man, whose work developed on a parallel trajectory to Derrida's. De Man's brand of deconstruction was a form of rhetorical analysis, an attempt to show that literary, critical, and philosophical arguments are invariably destabilized by the figures and tropes that they necessarily employ. Other prominent deconstructionists included de Man's Yale colleagues J. Hillis Miller and Barbara Johnson. Since 1987, debate on deconstruction has frequently been dominated by the "de Man affair," the posthumous discovery of some 170 articles written by de Man in Nazi-occupied Belgium for a collaborationist newspaper. One of these articles is explicitly anti-Semitic.

Différance: A Derridean neologism derived from the French verb *différer* ("to differ," "to defer"). It is shorthand for Derrida's radicalized version of Ferdinand de Saussure's seminal insight that language is a system of differences "without positive terms." *Différance* is a jackhammer that Derrida brings to bear on the foundational concepts of Western metaphysics. If there is a Derridean master term, this is it, although Derrida has tried to prevent it from hardening into one.

Genealogy: Foucault's later term, borrowed from Nietzsche, for his project of "writing the history of the present." Genealogy differs from **archaeology** primarily in the added attention it gives to the place of power in the fabric(ation) of truth and knowledge.

Intertextuality: Coined by Julia Kristeva, this term denotes the multiple ways in which one text echoes, rewrites, or is otherwise intertwined with other texts, whether through overt citation and allusion, or—and this is much more Kristevan—through the sheer fact of its forming a node in a network that, for all intents and purposes, is boundless. Each text is traversed by countless other texts independently of the agency of any one author. Derrida's theory of intertextuality, while largely implicit, has strong points of contact with Kristeva's, as does Roland Barthes's. Barthes singles out the reader, however, as the "place" where the innumerable cultural "quotations" that make up the text are inscribed. Foucault, for his part, shows how textual relations are imbricated with power relations; texts link up, not just with other texts, but with institutions, professions, systems of oppression, and so on. Foucault also demotes the author, however. In more recent theory, the challenge has been that of restoring a measure of agency to the author—especially in cases where factors such as race or gender have tended to strip the author of agency anyway—but without evading the poststructuralist critiques of traditional concepts of authorship and authorial "influence."

Logocentrism: Barbara Johnson tells it best: " 'Logocentric'—that which is centered on the 'Logos' (= speech, logic, reason, the Word of God)—is the term used by Derrida to characterize any signifying system governed by the notion of the self-presence of meaning; i.e., any system structured by a valorization of speech over writing, immediacy over distance, identity over difference, and (self-)presence over all forms of absence, ambiguity, simulation, substitution, or negativity" (translator's note in Derrida, *Dissemination*, 4).

Metaphysics of presence: What the Western intellectual tradition has always been obsessed with, according to Derrida. The expression is actually a pleonasm, since *metaphysics,* in Derridean usage, is shorthand for any system of thought that privileges presence.

Narrative criticism: A uniquely American form of biblical criticism, mainly holistic in thrust and associated with the study of the Gospels and Acts. It appropriates secular narratology (see **structuralism**) to analyze plot, character, point of view, setting, narrative time, and other features of Gospel narrative, including the intratextual reader (at which point it shades over into **reader-response criticism**). Narrative criticism has no precise analogue in nonbiblical literary criticism. It is not yet possible to speak of a poststructuralist narrative criticism, although some literary theorists have claimed that a poststructuralist narratology is conceivable.

Postmodernism: Variously defined as "a radical reader-oriented literary criticism" (Edgar V. McKnight); a "criticism which would include in its own discourse an implicit (or explicit) reflection upon itself" (Linda Hutcheon); a belated irruption in academic discourse, catalyzed by French poststructuralism, of the crisis of representation that marked the emergence of modernist art and literature more than a century ago (Andreas Huyssen); a mind-set that takes pleasure in the play of surfaces and derides the search for depth as mere nostalgia (Todd Gitlin); a skeptical interrogation of the "metanarratives" of universal progress inherited from the Enlightenment (Jean-François Lyotard); "a creative synthesis of modern and premodern truths and values" (David Ray Griffin); "a desire to think in terms sensitive to difference (of others without opposition, of heterogeneity without hierarchy)" (Hal Foster); "an acceptance of the challenge that other religious options present to the Judeo-Christian tradition; . . . a sense of the displacement of the white, Western male and the rise of those dispossessed due to gender, race, or class" (Sallie McFague); "not the cultural dominant of a wholly new social order . . . , but only the reflex and the concomitant of yet another systemic modification of capitalism itself" (Fredric Jameson).

Reader-Response Criticism: Less a unified method or theory than a spectrum of contrasting positions, some centered on the ways in which literary texts guide, educate, and manipulate their readers (New Testament reader-response critics fall mainly into this category), others more interested in how readers actually read (which may have little to do with subtle textual promptings), and still others centered on the factors that enable and delimit reading in the first place (competence, cultural or institutional location, gender, etc.). Is reader-response criticism a form of poststructuralism? Not usually, although there may be an overlap of interests. For example, Foucault's skepticism regarding "objects prior to discourse" finds an analogue in Stanley Fish's contention that all the formal properties of a text are purely the products of interpretation. A more general example would be **deconstruction**'s frequent fixation with the act of reading. But whereas the "stories of reading" told by reader-response critics usually have happy endings, those told by deconstructionists do not.

Signified: Ferdinand de Saussure's term for the conceptual component of the linguistic sign (e.g., the concept *tree*).

Signifier: Ferdinand de Saussure's term for the sensible or material component of the linguistic sign (e.g., the sound *tree*, or its appearance when written).

Structuralism: The application of explanatory principles derived from linguistics, preeminently those of Ferdinand de Saussure, to such fields as anthropology, literary studies, psychoanalysis, cultural studies, history, political science, and biblical studies. Literary structuralists, for example, attempt to elaborate general narrative "grammars," to specify the rules, codes, and conventions that govern the production of individual narratives. Whether studying mythology, tribal intermarriage, fashion magazines, or literature, structuralists are characteristically interested in moving from the particular to the general, from the individual instance to the underlying laws, from "surface structures" to "deep structures." Biblical structuralism, therefore, in its more ambitious forms, attempts to analyze biblical texts as products of transhistorical and transcultural generative systems, bracketing historical considerations in order to do so. Less ambitious forms of biblical structuralism seek to analyze the texts in terms of their "surface" components (actions, characters, settings, etc.)—at which point they shade over into **narrative criticism**. The latter is actually an offshoot of "narratology," the main form of literary structuralism.

Transcendental Signified: Derridean shorthand for any concept thought to transcend interpretation or signification in such a way as to ground, orient, stabilize, or end them (God, essence, identity, the author's intention, etc.). More generally, it would be any order of meaning assumed to be self-evident, self-identical, originary, final, or foundational.

AUTHOR AND SUBJECT INDEX

INDEX OF BIBLICAL AND OTHER ANCIENT SOURCES

Page numbers in italic designate an explicit interpretation of a verse or verses.

HEBREW BIBLE (OLD TESTAMENT)

Genesis

3:8	29
24:17	43

1 Samuel

16:7	110

1 Kings

8:39	110

2 Kings

17:13-34	47

1 Chronicles

28:9	110

Psalms

17:3	110
26:2	110
44:21	110
69:22	55
139:1-2	110
139:23	110

Proverbs

15:11	110

Isaiah

66:24	*105*

Jeremiah

11:20	110
12:3	110
17:10	110

NEW TESTAMENT

Matthew

27:35	*96*

Mark

15:24	*96*

Luke

15:3ff	51
16:23-26	*105*
23:33	*96*

John

1:1	29
1:7-9	45

1:10	45
1:18	45, 59
1:13	45
1:26	45
1:31	45
1:31-33	45
1:51	45, 59
2:6ff.	45
2:6-10	55
2:19-21	45
3:1ff.	*46*
3:3-4	45
3:4	*61*

OTHER ANCIENT WORKS